Publisher :
EASTERN BOOK LINKERS
5825, New Chandrawal, Jawahar Nagar,
Delhi-110007

Price RS. 300-

I Edition : 1996

ISBN : 81-86339-25-6

Printed at :
A.R. Printers, D-102 New Seelampur, DELHI-110053.

THE VEDA

And

VEDĀNTA

Ram Murti Sharma

Ph.D., D. Litt., F.R.A.S. (London)
Emeritus Fellow U.G.C.)
Department of Sanskrit, University of Delhi
Formerly, Professor & Head, Department of Sanskrit,
Punjab University, Chandigarh
National Lecturer & National Fellow (U.G.C.)
Recipient : President's Certificate of
Merit & Award.

Eastern Book Linkers

DELHI : : (India)

THE VEDA

AND

VEDĀNTA

Dedicated, with High Reverence,

to

Hon'ble Dr. Shanker Dayal Sharma,

The President of India,

a Scholar of global repute, a humanitarian,

an Apostle of Peace and Justice, a great

disciplinarian, a great patriot and

saviour of Indian Culture.

Foreword

Vedānta represents a high watermark of world philosophy, and has been the foundation for numerous philosophical systems in India down through the centuries. There are many interpretations of the great *Prasthānatrayī*, the three foundations of Vedānta comprising the Upaniṣads, the Bhagawadgītā and the Brahmasūtra. Ādi-Śaṅkarācārya's approach occupies a prominent place in our philosophical structure, and has provided a fertile field for research and interpretation by scholars in India and abroad. Prof. Ram Murti Sharma has presented a useful survey of Mukti thought and has given special attention to concepts such as and Akṣara.

(Dr.) Karan Singh

24 November, 1995

ABBRIVIATIONS

Abhi—Abhiprāyaprakāśikā

Aita—Aitareyabrāhmaṇa

AV—Atharva Veda

B.G. Bhagavadgītā

B.O.R.I.—Bhandarkar Orientel Research Institute, Poona

Bṛ—Bṛhadāraṇyakopaniṣad

B.S.S.B.—Brahmasūtraśāṅkarabhāṣya

Ch.—Chāndogyopaniṣad

G.K. – Gauḍapādakārikā

Iśa – Īśopaniṣad

Kaṭhā—Kaṭhopaniṣad

Muṇḍ—Muṇḍakopaniṣad

N.S.—Naiṣkarmyasiddhi

RV—Ṛgveda

S.B.—Śatapathabrāhmaṇa

S.B.E. – Sacred Books of the East

S.B.G.—Śāṅkarabhāṣya Gītā

S.K.—Sāṅkhyakārikā

Śvet. – Śvetāṣvataropaniṣad

Taitti.—Taittirīyopaniṣad

V.P.—Viṣṇupurāṇa

YV—Yajurveda

Preface

The Veda and Vedānta, are two highly significant branches of indological learning and if Veda can be said as the main base of the Vedānta, the later is the philosophic conclusion of the former. It may be said that the Vedic studies without Vedāntic purview will remain unexplained and incomplete. The two are co-ordinating and inseparable and therefore it has been felt necessary, to study them from the aforesaid viewpoint. The Vedānta is an overall complete thought, which has its linkage with other systems of philosophy and has an impact on most of them. Not only as a philosophical system, its supremacy is recognized throughout the whole world, it has also been studied with its social relevance, as a practical vedānta, in India and abroad. In this country, particularly practical Vedānta of Vivekānanda and a number of other neo-vedāntins, has brought to notice the utility of Vedānta from the viewpoint of social relevance. For the day is full of various types of myseries caused of domestic and social conflicts, due to moral lacuna, and social and economic inequities, there is felt a need of studying and understanding Vedānta in the whole globe and therfore its readership has gone highly up in east and west. In this context, present author is happy that his fellowship has been inspired by the readers of Vedānta, to read and recognize his works, like Śaṅkarācārya, Advaita Vedānta, Some aspects of Advaita philosophy, Glimpses of Vedānta, the Vedāntasāra (ed.) and the Encyclopaedia of Vedānta. I am highly thankful to them all. In India, along with moral, cultural and philosophical heritage, the saints of Vedic and post-Vedic period and onward, have impressed upon the whole human kind, through their saintliness, full of human-kindness, venevolence, attitude of human-welfare and overall goodness. It is worth-mentioning that the base of sainthood in India, is Śaṅkarite Vedānta, and Vaiṣṇavite both, particularly the Advita Vedāntā of Śaṅkara. Nānaka, Kabīra, Jñāneśvara, Mīrā and many others may be referred to in this regard. In modern era, the saints, like Sister Nivedita, Mother of Pondicherry, Maharṣi Ramaṇa and Mother Teressa have done a great service for the welfare of human beings. This aspect too has been taken up in the present study.

Former Union Minister and Ambassador to the United States of America, Dr. Karan Singh has been very kind to contribute his foreword to the present volume. I am highly grateful to him. Indeed, a word, from a scholar and advocate of international repute in the field of Vedānta, like Dr. Karan Singh, is of a great value to me and I am further indebted for his sincere affection towards me.

I am sincerely thankful to learned professor (Miss) Armaiti S. Desai, Chairperson and Professor Y.C. Mathur, Vice-Chairman, University grants commission for encouraging me in my pursuit of studies.

The idea of collecting the thread of above mentioned views and to interweave them came after organizing four seminars, on Veda-Vedānta conflict resolution in the University of Delhi under the auspices of Dharam Hinduja International centre of Indic research, New Delhi, which is engaged In Vedic and Vedāntic research genuinely I am thankful to Dr. Kireet Joshi, President of DHICIR for giving me an opportunity to organize the said seminars. I also thank Dr. R.K. Sharma. Director of DHICIR and Mr. Ram Lal Arora, Administrative Officer of the Centre, for sharing the responsibility of organizing these seminars.

I specially thank my wife, Mrs. Chetan Sharma for allways giving me her hand in my academic pursuits. I can never repay her debt. I also thank my daughter Dr. Priti Sharma for contributing her paper, "Abhiprāya Prakāśikā and Brahman", to this volume: Dr. Vipul Gupta, a Ph.D.

Research scholar and my son, Mr. Abhishek Sharma, a student of M. Tech (BHU), who have helped me in preparing. the index. I wish them all a great success in their career.

Deputy Librarian, Mr. R. S. Saini, Mr. Sher Singh and Dr. J B. Khanna and other staff members of the Delhi University Library deserve special thanks, because, it is they who solved my problems regarding precuring me the very rare and precious treasure, I needed time to time.

In the end, I am thankful to Mr. Shyam Malhotra, Manager, EBL, for allways taking up my work to bring it out with keen interest and great zeal.

Guru Pūrṇimā, 1995

Manidweepa,

Shalimar Bagh, Delhi — Ram Murti Sharma

Introduction

The Veda has a unique place in the field of indology, because of the knowledge it contains on history, philosophy, metaphysics, science, mathematics, geography, literary elements, medicinal science and so on. The Vedic knowledge is the outcome of the revelations of the Ṛṣis, who because of their austeric power had revealed the innumerable screts of knowledge which have come to us through Śravaṇa tradition (Śruti-paramparā). The Veda is a reservoir of knowledge, which has numerous branches of which some have come to light and some are still untraced, because of insufficient researches and its vast and very deep scope area, albiet the ancient and modern scholars of the east and west, have made researches in various areas of Vedic researches. It is also a fact that in the later half of this century, there has been a special attention to the study of the Vedas, with a scientific approach, especially from the point of view of mathematics, physics, astrophysics, astronomy and sociology and scholars' interest in these areas has been gradually increasing due to very encouraging results achieved therein. However. it may be further emphasized that there is a much more need for making higher and specialized research in Vedic domain.

The Vedic Vāṅmaya includes, the four Saṁhitās, Ṛgveda. Yajurveda, Sāmaveda and Atharvaveda, the Upaniṣads, the Brāhmaṇas, the Āraṇyakas and the Śrautasūtras, mainly. As initiated at the outset, the Veda also contains science and technology, nonconventional sources of energy, and the weather science.

The scientific approach also can be made to the study of Vedānta. *In this respect,* the physisist scholars like Dr. Raja Ramanna have successfully done it. As far as the philosophical part of the Veda is concerned, it is related to Mīmāṃsā

(Karma Kāṇḍa) and the Uttaramīmāṃsā (Jñānakāṇḍa). The Karmakāṇḍa is a prior aspect of Jñānakāṇḍa, which is the final doctrine of the Veda and therefore it is rightly said as Vedānta. Now, it may be mentioned that the whole structure of Vedānta is based on the tenet of Br hman, which is propounded as non-dual, infinite and as an ultimate reality. How this Advaitic theory of reality is prevalant in the Saṃhitās, is to be seen here. To my mind, the Ṛgvedic thoughts of one reality (Ekamsad viprā vahudhā vadanti) is the core idea of the whole of the Vedic thought, which presents a clear background for the Advaitic standpoint. Furthermore, the indescribable entity described in the RV (Nā-sadāsīt no sadāsīt tadānīm), the Puruṣa of the Puruṣa-sūkta, who is the Lord of immortality, and has been described as the universal soul, the Hirainyagarbha, who is the Godhead, as the great power of the universe, the Viśvakarmā, described as the creator and controller of the universal creation, the Vāk, described as the substratum of the whole universe, and the Bṛhaspati or Brahmaṇaspati, the creator, is clearly indicative of the Advaitic origin. Needless to say that these points are related to procreation which is a part of philosophy. It may further be mentioned that the "Tapas" of the Nāsadīyasūkta which has been described as the cause of creation, is "Saṁkalpa" of the Lord. This idea is prominently elaborated in the Upaniṣadic expressions, like "Eko' haṃ vahu-syām". It is also necessary to note the Ṛg-Vedic panthiesm and the style of addressing a God, as for the time being, the God with an entire forgetfulness of other Gods, is also indicative of the later Advaitic standpoint. In the Yajurveda, Prajāpati, Brahman and Puruṣa, are prevalent for the same meaning. In the Sāma-Veda Saṃhitā (vi. 3.17) also, there is an expression which mentions about Brahman, the causal entity : "Tadihāsa bhuvaneṣu jyeṣṭham". Here Sāyaṇa means Brahman, the causal entity, by the word "tat". The same way, in the A.V. There is a clear description of Brahman as substratum and of the world as superimposed and thus this is fully evident of the Advaitic doctrine. Furthermore, in the Atharvaveda, Brahman is identified with Kāla (Time) and this Kāla is the cause of the whole cosmos. There is similarity, between Ṛta and Kāla, because both are moving and the deities are described as born and increased by Ṛta and thus they are said as Ṛtajāta and Ṛtavṛddha.

So also, in the Brāhmaṇas and the Āraṇyakas, Brahman, the key principle of Vedānta finds a prominent place. In the Śatapatha, epitomically, Brahman has been mentioned as Svayambhūḥ, Virāṭ and the cause of creation. The use of the word, Brahmavādin and Brahmavit in the Taittirīyabrāhmaṇa, further indicates about the concept of Brahman. In the Āraṇyakas too, the Brahmanic thoughts are prevalant. To illustrate, Aitareyāraṇyaka describes Satcidānanda Paramātman as the cause of creation and Ātman as an allpervading entity. The Taittirīyarāṇyaka says that after creating the universe, Paramātman entered in it. Describing the Advaitic characteristic of Brahman, the Śāṅkhāyana mentions Ātman as Brahman and Brahman as Apūrva, Apara, Anapara and Abhaya.

The above chain of Brahmanic thought of the Vedic literature gets concentrated in the Upaniṣads. Therein, more particularly in the Chāndogyopaniṣad, Brahman has been propounded as a supreme and ultimate reality and an allpervading entity. It is further described as determinate and indeterminate. Logically it seems that it was done, for justifying the universal creation, from the determinate who is the efficient cause of the cosmos due to His Māyā Śakti as well as its overall controller. It was not justifiable with immutable Brahman, which is a nameless and formless entity. At this stage, it is remarkable that the role of Māyā in the Upaniṣadic and later philosophical thought is highly significant. Accordingly from the point of view of creation, its sustenance, controlling and dissolution, and the state and functioning of individual soul, the doctrine of Māyā is highly important, for it is due to the adjunct of Avidyā or Māyā that the pure soul takes the form of individual soul (Jīva) and it experiences the result of the deeds.

It is noteworthy that the Upaniṣads describe Brahman and Ātman as the same (Ayamātmā brahma) and also state that Brahman which is Jñāna is not different from Mokṣa (Brahmaiva muktyavasthā and thus, as the Upaniṣads doctrinize, Brahman itself is the state of Mukti. It is therefore, that according to the Upaniṣads the knower of Brahman, the Brahmavit, becomes Brahman. Tnking in view the practicability of Brahma-Jñāna, the Upaniṣads clearly hint at the idea of Jivānmukti and Videhamukti, although not in a very distinguished manner. For example, when it is said in the Chāndogyopaniṣad that as water does not cl ng to the leaf of lotus, likewise evıl does not cling to one who knows Brahman (Ch. iv. 14.3). Also the Bṛhadāraṇyakopaniṣad says that as the slough of a snake lies on an anthill dead cast off, even so this body of this disembodied immortal life is Brahman only (Bṛha. ix. 7.7). These ideas are clearly indicative of the concept of Jīvanmukti. About the Videhamukti, the Kaṭhopaniṣad says that the liberated leaves this body and he never takes rebirth. (Vimuktaśca vimucyate). Thus the Upaniṣadic thought is a clear network of the later Vedāntic system which was formulated first by Gauḍapāda and thereafter by Śaṅkara, the forepiller of Advaitā philosophy.

Gauḍapādācārya, the grand guru of Śaṅkarācārya, having rich background of Vedāntic literature, i.e. the Upaniṣads, the Bhagwadgītā, the Brahmasūtra and the Yogavāśiṣṭha in the four Prakaraṇas—Āgama, Vaitathya. Advaita and Alātaśānti of his Gauḍapākārikā or known as the Māṇḍkya Kārikā, propounded the tenet of Advaita with the support of his concept of unborn (Ajāti), which proved that the world is really unborn and it is falsely born due to Māyā. "Sato hi Māyayā Janma yujyate na tu tattvataḥ" This is known as the Ajātavāda doctrine of the Gauḍapādakārikā. To pexplain the falsehood of the world, Gauḍapādācārya, used mainly the similies of dream, Gandharvanagara and the son of a barren woman (Vandhyāputra), which seems to be a Buddhistic influence. In Alātaśānti prakaraṇa of the Kārikā, the Ācārya describes at length, that the firebrands of a burning wheel appear to be distinct and real, while they are mere appearances. According to Gauḍapādācārya, the duality of the individual souls and the world, stands, till a person is not able to realize the nondual reality, Brahman. When it is known, the duality completely ends and this is said as the state of Advaitic realization (Advaita-bhāva). Thus, Gauḍapādācārya is a prime Advaitin, prior to Śaṅkarācārya, who advocated his philosophy of Ajātavāda in a conceptual manner.

Śaṅkarācārya, the main architect and chief enunciator of Advaita-vāda established his philosophical doctrine, not avoiding the schools and tenets of other philosophical systems. Thus he propounded his Advaitic doctrine, taking critically into full consideration, the Nyāya, the Vaiśeṣika, the Sāṃkhya, the Yoga, the Bauddha, the Jaina, the Kāpālika and the Śaivaite schools. He, keeping in view, the philosophical concepts of most of the above systems and refuting them with logical arguments in his Brahmasūtrābhāṣya presented the full structure of Advaita philosophy and raised it to the peak state of thought, which was recognised, accepted and praised throughout in the east and west. It will not be too much to say that the Vedānta advocated by Sāṅkara, is the best known Indian school of philosophy in the whole globe. It is the most significant contribution of the philosophy of Śaṅkarācārya that he expounded the Advaitic thought in the full doctrinal form with the help of doctrine of Māyā. He emphasized on the Anirvacanīya character of Māyā and elaborated that the Māyic world also is Anirvacanīya and thus not entirely false. Śaṅkara very much takes the world as subject to experince (vyavahāra), because of its phenomenal character. He advocates non-duality between Brahman, Jīva and the world, on the basis of substratum and superimposition, according to which Brahman is the substratum (Adhiṣṭhāna) and the world is superimposition (Adhyāsa). It is just like the snake super-imposed on rope or silver superimposed on conchshell.

Regarding the individual characteristic of Jīva, Śaṅkarācārya said that it is pure Ātman who takes the form of Jīvahood, due to the adjunct of Avidyā. As soon as Avidyā is removed through the knowledge of infinite (Brahmajñāna), the Jīva becomes Brahman (Jīvo Brhmaiva nāparaḥ) and this is said as the state of release from the bondage of the dual world. Śaṅkarācārya, very much supports the concept of Jīvanmukti and Videhamukti and the former is quite meaningful from the view point of practicability and social relevance of Advaita philosophy. The Advaita Vedānta of Śaṅkara has been further expounded and commented by several Ācāryas like Sureśvara, Padmapāda, Vācaspatimiśra and so on.

For a Jīvanmukta is samadarśin, to him, all are equal in society. As the Vedānta advocates the philosophy of Ekātmavāda, there is no scope for the feeling of caste and creed. In the Brahmasūtra-bhāṣya, Śaṅkarācārya clearly mentions that the Ātmatattva has no concern with the caste like Brāhmaṇa, Kṣatriya etc, 'Apeta-brahma Kṣatrādibhedamātmatattvam'. It is because of various adjuncts, that one has the feeling of caste and creed etc., Śaṅkara says in his Ātmabodha. Thus from the view point of global unity and human service, the Vedānta is of utmost importance. It is the foreground of the idea of common-wealth of humanity which should be shared by all, having the sense of human kindness and world brotherhood. In this manner this Advaita Vedānta formulates the concept of an ideal man who has no attachment, no selfishness and lives a life of dignity and freedom and he is allways for social and economic-equality and human welfare, because in him, he has the ground of Ekātmavāda. Thus the Advaita Vedānta presents a clear picture of an ideal man, who is for par excilence in this world. It is the true concept of man according to Vedānta. An ideal man's best achievement is human fellowship and his supreme attainment is peace which is allways blissful. The concept of man has also been presented by the Greek, the Jewish, the Indian and the Chinese tradition. Of them, the first three have been analysed by king John Wild of Harvard University, A.J. Hischel of New York (USA), and Dr. S. Radha krishnan and P.T. Rajus, the eminent Indian scholars, respectively. While analysing the Greek philosophy, John Wild has taken into account the seminal significance of Socretes, Plato and Aristotle and has found the influence of the Greek thought on various religious traditions. So also Haschel of the Jewish Seminary of New York, examining the Jewish thought, has taken in view the meaning of existence, the necessity of accepting God, the paradox of divine concern and man as the symbol of God. Viwing upon the Indian concept of man, P.T. Raju has based it on Vedic concept of man and the concept of Jainism and Buddhism and epics as well as some other orthodox schools. It may be pointed oui that the tenets like non-violence of Janism and Buddhism are originally based on the one soul theory of the Upaniṣadic Vedānta. Thus the Vedānta can be said as the basic mannual of human conduct and behaviour. Accordingly it was brought into practice by saints like Swāmi Rāmakṛṣṇa Pramahaṃsa and many others. This makes clear the social relevance of Śaṅkarite Vedānta. Viewing its social significance, an American scholar Clooney S.J. suggests "Second, sooner rather than later, we need to undertake some case studies, ancient or modern, comparative, or drawn solely from the Indian context, in which we can begin to see how Vedānta has upto now mattered in situation of conflict. But at first reflection it is difficult to see what such a case study might look like since there are surely four situations, ancient or modern, in which any one has applied Vedānta directly to situations of conflict" Vedānta and conflict resolution, (unpublished paper, Page 29, Boston College, USA, March, 199-). Regarding this, typical suggestion, it may be said that in this country, India, innumerable saints and philosophers, followers of Vedāntic way, since long India's past and so also innumerable Indian families have been living more or less peacefully, having an impact of Vedāntic views. In fact Vedāntic understanding is in the clay of this land and thus even a layman talks of Vedāntic ideas, like, the Lord is an overall controller and that the world is Māyā. Another American scholar Kaplan's sociological forecast that "Conflict in the 21st century will be more akin to crime than war, and we will need to take into account endemic and more invisible forms of violence ranging from domestic abuse to vast economic inequities," (The coming Anarchy, (article) published in the Atlantic Monthly, Feb. 1994). Here it is to be said that the Vedāntic view of life will always be a source of solace to humankind and thus it is a universal and eternal remedy to man, which may cope with various situations arising due to many inequities in society. About the practicability of Vedānta, it will be proper to know the views of another American scholar, Wilhelm Halbfass, who says : "It would not be difficult to complete literally hundreds of statements asserting that Advaita Vedānta has practical i.e. ethical, social and political relevance for India as well as an even more fundamental relevance for the future of all mankind. It has been invoked against poverty, injustice and the dangers of the nuclear age" (Karan Singh) It has been associated with such concepts as tolerance, equality, peaceful co-existence, brotherhood, internationalism, the community of nations, democracy, the social and economic justice as well as with proclamations of cultural or national identity and superiority, Utopian notions of anarchy and so forth". ("Practical Vedânta" : Some observations and questions, Page 2-3 unpublished paper by Wilhelm Haltfass.) Thus the Advaitic view is a remedy to psycological, social and the evils of economic inequity as well as the religious imbalances and with it one can lead a happy and peaceful life.

R.M.S.

Contents

Vedic Cosmogony

An inquisitiveness to Vedic cosmogony is natural, because of its ancientness, mysterious expressions and dealing with creation of the cosmos. In fact, it precedes the quest for knowing the reality, the essence and the universe, and which obviously covers the problems, such as creation, phenomenality and spiritualism. Therefore it is, that Bādarāyaṇa begins his Brahmasūtra, with an enquiry into Brahman (Athāto Brahmajijñāsā). Thus Vedic cosmogony comes within the purview of philosophy which may be said as an eye to know and realize the reality of phenomenal as well as spiritual life and may be admitted as the pathway for achieving the best objective of mankind, the liberation. Therefore it is imperative that the earliest and oldest revealers of the essence of life and truth, the Vedas, particularly the Ṛgveda, contains the rich philosophical thoughts which make a firm foundation for the later philosophical literature. As far as the Ṛgveda is concerned, it embodies a great deal of philosophical elements. Thus in the RV, many hymns like Nāsadīya, Puruṣa & Hiraṇyagarbha, contain the views on cosmogony, an integral part of philosophy, and a study of the cosmogonic perspectives in the RV may be made on the basis of the Ṛgvedic text which reveals the ideas related to truth of life, human objective, creation as well as religion. Accordingly herein, to properly analyse the cosmogonic perspectives of the Ṛgvedic text, textual expressions regarding the Ṛgvedic ideas on reality (Sat), the Nāsadīya hymn, the Puruṣa hymn and such others are to be introspected.

Alongwith the RV, as would be quite appropriate, the cosmogonic ideas in the Yajurveda, The Atharvaveda, The Brāhmaṇas and the Upaniṣads, will also be viewed upon.

Besides, the interpretation of Paṇḍit Madhusūdana Ojhā, on cosmogony, will be presented.

The Ṛgvedic View

As regards the idea of reality, the Ṛgvedic text—"Ekam sad viprā vahudhā vadanti,"[1] mentions that the one reality is expressed in many ways by the scholars. But at another place, the unreal (Asat) has been said as the cause of real (Sat), the universal creation.[2] Here the contradiction in the above two statements, is apparent. But, if the above two statements are understood in a proper philosophical perspective, there remains no scope for contradiction. To argue and elaborate, it may be said that while the Sat, in the hymn, "Ekam sad viprā Bahudhā vadanti" has been mentioned as the base of all, it only means the subtle reality, which is without name and form, Explaining this reality, Sāyaṇa says: "Amumeva Ādityamekamevavastutaḥ Santam vipra medhāvino devatātattvavido vahudhā vadanti" Tat tat kāryakāraṇena Indrādyātmānam vadanti. Ekaivava mahānātmödevatā so sūrya ityācakṣata.[3] As far as the above Ṛgvedic statement regarding the Asat for mentioning it, as the origin of the universe is concerned, it (Asat) is to be appropriately understood for non-apparent Sat, which is apparently Asat, but in subtility, Sat. Therefore, if the above mentioned two Ṛgvedic expressions are properly understood, the contradiction cannot he justified. Thus it may be said that if the Ṛgvedic philosophical text is not understood, having in mind the overall context, composit and compact view, it may mislead.

In the above context of Ṛgvedic Sat and Asat, the Nāsadīyasūkta is of great importance, which reads thus :

---

1. Ṛgveda, 1.164.46.
2. Devānām pūrve yuge asataḥ sadajāyata. Ṛgveda, V.X. 72.
3. Ṛgveda, 1.164.46.

1. nāsad āsin, no sad āsit tadānim;
nāsid rajo no viomā paro yat.
kim āvarīvaḥ ? kuha sārmann ?
ambhaḥ kim asid, gahanam gabhīram ?

2. na mṛtyur āsīd, amṛtam na tarhi.
na rātriā ahna āsīt praketaḥ.
āsīd avātam svadhayā tad ekam.
tasmād dhānyan na parah kim canāsa.

3. tama āsīt tamasā guḍham agre;
aparaketam salilam sarvam ā idam.
tuchyenābhū apihitamyad āsīt,
tapasas tan mahinājāyataikam.

4. kāmas tad agre sam avartatādhi,
manaso retaḥ prathamam yad āsīt.
sato bandhum asati nir-avindan
hṛdi pratīṣya kavayo manīṣā.

5. tiraścīno vitato raśmir eṣām :
adhaḥ svid āsīd, upari svid āsīt ?
retodha āsan mahimāna āsan ;
svadhā avastāt, prayatiḥ parastāt

6. ko adddhā veda ka iha pra vocat,
kuta ājāta, kuta iyam visṛṣṭih ?
arvāg devā asya visarjanena :
atha ko veda yata ababhūva ?

7. iyam viṣṛṣṭir yata ābabhūva ;
yadi vā dadhe yadi vā na :
yo asyādhyakśaḥ paramo vioman
so anga veda, yadi vā na veda.

Through the Nāsadīya sūkta, it is affirmed that in the beginning, there was neither Sat nor Asat, but different from both and thus some Anirvacanīya (indescribable) entity, as elaborated in Vedānta literature. Thus according to the

Nāsadīya hymn, which explains the beginning of creation, the reality was neither existent (Sat) and nor non-existent (Asat). It means that the reality is neither apparently existent and nor non-existent, because it was subtle in its basic state. Thus, here, if the meaning of Sat is understood properly, there can not be established any contradiction, between Sat and Asat. In this regard, an expression in the hymn, "Sato bandhu-masati nirabindan" (The cause of Sat was found in Asat) is to be viewed upon. In it, the meaning of Asat has been taken as Abhāva (non-existent) by certain scholars like Peterson who translates the part of the Mantra thus : "Sages who searched with their heart's thought discovered the existent's kinship in the non-existent".[1] Here, to interpret "Asat" as non-existent, is not proper because, nothing can be originated from Asat (not existent). Thus the above interpretation of Asat as non-existent is without keeping in view the overall context of the Ṛgvedic philosophical persepctive, particularly creative process, which hints "Sat" as the origin of creation, as said above. In this connection, Macdonell is correct, when he comments upon to say "They found the origin of the evolved world in the unevolved."[2] In fact, the unevolved is subtle reality. This is similar to the spirit of "Ekam sad Viprā Bahudhā Vadanti." The term "Yataḥ" in the expressions, "Iyaṃ visṛṣṭi-ryata ābabhūva[3] "Yto vāimāni bhūtāni Jāyante"[4] and "Janmādyasya-yataḥ"[5] further indicates towards the causal reality, the unmanifest Sat. In another example of the Ṛgvedic text, in the expression, "Tapasaḥ mahinā ajāyata" the term tapas is to be interpreted as self effulgent Tapas (Saṅkalpa) of God.

---

1. Peterson, The hymns of the Ṛgveda, P. 575.
2. A Vedic reader, P. 209.
3. Ṛgveda X.129.7
4. Taittirīyopaniṣad, III, 1.1 .
5. Brahmasūtra, 1.1.2.

In this context, Macdonell's interpretation "that one arose through the process of heat"[1] is not at all convincing. Also Peterson's understanding of "Warmth"[2] by the term "Tapas is not proper, because Tapas" of God (Unseen) is a form of "Saṁkalpa" Wilson translates "Tapas" Thus : 'Austerity' meaning the contemplation of the things that were to be created.[3] "Burnouf in his La science des religious (PP 207, shows that how warmth was regarded by Āryans as the principle explaining movement, life and thought. At this juncture, Sāyaṇa's following interpretation is quite meaningful :

> "Bhāvarūpājñānamātratama ityucyate. Tapasaḥ sraṣṭavya-paryālocanarūpasya māhātmyena ajāyata. (Sāyaṇabhāṣya, Ṛgveda, X. 129.3.)

The interpretation of "Tapas" as "Saṁkalpa" is further proved in the Upaniṣadic thought, where God had the desire (Saṁkalpa) of becoming many (Saḥ akāmayata bahusyām prajāyeya iti"[4] This view also can be witnessed in the earliest commentary of the Nāsadīya, the Śatapatha Brāmana.[5] It is thus : In the beginning, this (Universe) was as it existed and did not exist : there was then only this Mind. Wherefor it has been declared by the Ṛṣi (Ṛgveda, X. 129.1). "There was then neither the non-existent nor the existent" for mind was, as it were, neither existent nor non-existent. This mind when created, wished to become manifest,—more defined, more substantial : it sought after a self (a body); it practised austerity : it acquired consistency.

1. A Vedic reader, p. 209.
2. The Hymns of the Ṛgveda. p. 55.
3. See, Peterson's the Hymns of the Ṛgveda p. 575.
4. Taittirīyopaniṣad, II, 6.
5. See, Śatapatha Brāhmaṇa, X.V. 3.1 and Eggeling's translation, S.B.E. Vol. XL. III, pp. 374, 375. See also, Atharvaveda, X. 7.10.

The above mentioned ideas of the Nāsadīyasūkta can be said as the basics of vedic cosmogony.

While taking in view the cosmogonic perspective of the Ṛgvedic text, our attention is unavoidably drawn to the Puruṣa hymn (Puruṣa Sūkta), the foremost philosophical hymn of the RV. The Puruṣa Sūkta reads thus :

1. Puruṣa evedam sarvam
yadbhūtam yac ca bhāviam
utāmrtatvasyeśāno,
yadannenātirohati.

2. etāvan asya mahimā,
ato jyāyaṁś ca Puruṣah.
pādo 'sya viśvā bhūtāni;
tripād asyāmṛtam divi.

3. tripād ūrdhva ud ait Puruṣaḥ;
pādo 'syehābhavat punaḥ.
tato viśvaṅ vi akrāmat
sāśanānaśane abhi.

4. tasmād Virāḍ ajāyata,
Virājo adhi puruṣaḥ.
sa jāto aty aricyata
Paścād bhūmim atho puraḥ.

5. yat Puruṣeṇa haviṣā
devā yajñam atanvata,
vasanto asyāsīd ājyam
grīṣma idhmaḥ, śarad dhaviḥ.

6. tam yajñam barhisi parukṣan
Puruṣam Jātam agrataḥ :
tena devā ayajanta,
sādhyā ṛṣayaś ca ye.

7. tasmad yajñāt sarvahutaḥ
sambhṛtam pṛṣadājiam :

paśūṅ tāṁś cakre vāyavyān,
āraṇyān, grāmiaś ca ye.

8. tasmād yajñāt sarvahuta
ṛeaḥ sāmāni jajñire;
chandāṁsi jajñire tasmād;
yajus tasmād ajāyata.

9. tasmād aśvā ajāyanta, ye ke ca ubhayādataḥ.
gāvo ha jaiṅire tasmāt;
tasmāj jātā jāvayaḥ.

10. yat Puruṣam viadadhuḥ,
katidha vi akalpayan ?
mukham kim asya ? kau bāhū ?
kā ūrū pādā ucyete ?

11. brāhmaṇo 'sya mukhaṁ āsīd,
bāhū rājaniaḥ krtaḥ;
ūrū tad asya yad vaiśyaḥ;
padbhyām śūdro ajāyata.

The Puruṣa Sūkta, the hymn of supreme soul is the only Sūkta which presents a clear view of the one universal and supreme reality, which is all pervading, in a systematic manner, to say that the Puruṣa has hundred heads, hundred eyes and hundred feet and that he having covered the earth on all sides, extended beyond it the length of ten figures. The Sūkta further says that Puruṣa is this all, that has been and that will be and he is the Lord of immortality.[1] In this thought, the clear seeds of the upaniṣadic and later Vedāntic view may be seen.

As has been mentioned at the outset, for analysing the philosophical cosmogonic perspective of the Ṛgvedic text, it is essential to keep in view the essence of the full hymn and

---

1. Puruṣa eveidam Sarvam yad bhūtam yacca bhāvyam.
Utāmṛtattvasye-śāno yadanonātirohati RV. X. 90.2.

the overall philosophical purview of the RV. In its absence, an interpretation will be futile, as may be seen in the example of the Puruṣa sūkta. Macdonell has translated the Puruṣa of the Puruṣa Sūkta, as man.[1] In this regard, Peterson's interpretation is quite appropriate, while he interprets the Puruṣa as a "Universal" soul."[2] Regarding Puruṣa Macdonells" explanation is further to be examined, when he says "while the material out of which the world is made is the body of a primaeval giant named Puruṣa."[3] Here, to interpret the Puruṣa as "material for making the world" is not appropriate. Indeed the Puruṣa Sūkta should be studied in the line of the view of one reality (Ekam-Sad viprā Bahudhā Vadanti.") and the Nāsadīya Sūkta, wherein, the cause has been mentioned as different from Sat and Asat both. Thus, to take Puruṣa as "material" does not seem to have a proper sense. Furthermore Macdonell's opinion "The religious view" is moreover different from that of the old hymns, for it is pantheistic. Puruṣa is all this world, what has been and shall be"[4] also does not stand with reason. It is because the old hymns' view of one reality. (Ekam sat viprā Bahudhā vadanti) and the view of the Nāsadīya Sūkta is not different from the religious view with pantheistic approach, for the Pantheism of the Puruṣa-sūkta, in a way, is a mythological explanation of the concept of one reality concept prevalent is the Ṛgveda.

Viewing upon the Puruṣa sūkta, Peterson says that the Puruṣa of the Puruṣa sūkta is "universal soul and he pervades the Universe, as the Individual soul he is enclosed in a space of narrow dimensions".[5] This view is similar to the later

1. A Vedic Reader, P. 195.
2. The Hymns of the Ṛgveda, p. 517.
3. A Vedic Reader, p. 195.
4. A Vedic Reader, p. 195.
5. See also, The Hymns of the Atharvaveda XIX. VI. 1, note.

view of Upaniṣadic vedānta, which enunciates that Brāhmaṇ is without the ajunct of Māyā and it is Individual soul, while it is adjuncted with Avidyā.

From the philosophical point of view the following verse of the Puruṣa Sūkta is significant :

"Puruṣa evedam sarvam, yad bhūtam yacca bhāvyam, utāmṛtattvasyeśāno yadannenātirohati."

Accordingly the Puruṣa is this all, that has been and that will be. And he is the Lord of immorality which he grows beyond through food. As Peterson interprets, "he is the Lord of immortality or the immortal world of Gods, which grows greater by food, that is, by the sacrificial offerings of men."[1] Wilson interprets it in a different way and says that "he is also the Lord of immortality; for he mounts beyond (his own condition), for the food of living beings."[2] Colebrook further takes it a bit differently and says "he is that which grows by nourishment and he is the distributor of immortality."[3] Dr. Muir's interpretation in this regard, is "He is also the Lord of immortality, since by food he expands."[4] Prof. Ludwig interprets it to say "auch uber die unsterblichkeit gebietend was durch speise meit ube vagt".[5] Accordingly he rules over immortality, since he far transcends what exists through food. Here, Sāyaṇa's interpretation is quite clear and exhaustive, when he says that he is the Lord or distributor of immortality, because, he becomes the visible world in order that living beings may obtain the fruits of their actions and gain Mokṣa or final liberation from their bonds." Needless to say, that all these interpretations have gone far from the text and it is quite in the fitness of things,

1. The Hymns of the Ṛgveda, p. 519.
2. The Ṛgveda, Puruṣa Sūkta, X. 90.2.
3. See, Peterson, The Hymns of the Ṛgveda, p 518.

4&5. *Ibid*, p. 518.

because words can speak only upto a limit. What I can say is that to take the proper philosophical & cosmogonic perspective of the text, one has to keep in mind the idea that Puruṣa, (the God) desired to express himself in the form of manifold world and it was his nature or Svabhāva. The same seed-like idea can be seen in the Nāsadīya Sūkta "Kāmastadagre samavartata".[1] As also said earlier, this view is frequently found in the Upaniṣads, (So 'Kāmayata vahusyām Prajāyeya)[2] and early Vedānta (Devasyaiṣa svabhāvo 'yam aptakāmasya kā spṛhā."[3] In the aforesaid Mantra, the term "Amṛtattva" also has been inerpreted differently, Macdonell & Peterson take it for immortality or Godliness." To some, it means water, nector and Mokṣa. On it Sāyaṇa comments:

> Utāpi cāmṛtattvasya devatvasyāyamīśānaḥ swāmī yadyasmaī kārṇāt annena prāṇinām bhaumyenānnena nimitta bhutenātirohati svakīyām kāraṇāvasthāmati k-ramya

paridṛṣya-mānām jagadāvasthām prāpnoti tasmāt prāminām karmaphala-bhogāya jagadavasthā svīkārānnedam tasya vastutvamityarthaḥ.

In all them, immortality as the meaning of "Amṛtattva" seems quite appropriate, because Puruṣa, is the Lord of immortality. By these specimen of the two hymns, the Nāsadīya and Puruṣa, it is evident that the philosophical and cosmogonic perspective of the Ṛgvedic text can be understood properly, if it is interpreted keeping in view the grammatical and linguistic peculiarities and analysed having in mind the contextual references and an overview of the Ṛgvedic philosophical thought as well as religious and social traditions. Needless to say that there is a need of taking into

1. Ṛgveda, X. 129.4.
2. Taittirīyopraniṣad II. e.
3. Gauḍapādakārikā, Āgamaprakarāṇa.

account the cosmogonic perspective of the hymns like Hiraṇyagarbha, Vāk & Vṛhaspati in the above manner and with an analytical approach.

The Hiraṇyagaibha hymna is much more meaningful from the stand-point of cosmogonic analysis. As it says, in the beginning, it was only Hiraṇyagarbha, which has been interpreted by the scholars in various manners. Accordingly Hiraṇyagarbha means, literally, the gold germ; source of golden light; the God 'as the great power of the universe, from which all other powers and existences, divine and earthly, are derived, a conception which is the nearest approach to the later mystrical conception of Brahmā, the creator of the world, as Walis says Peterson interprets Hiraṇyagarbha as Golden seed. So also' 'Samavartata' has been interpreted distinctly, in the Hiranyagarbha hymns. By 'Samavartata' Sāyaṇa means 'originated', Ubbata understands 'got embodied in the very beginning' and Mahīdhara interprets that the Hiranyagarbha "himself got embodied". The term "Kasmai" (for whom) also has been interpreted with a difference. Generally, it is interpreted thus : Ka means who? that is the unknown God, has been applied as a name to Prajāpati and to other gods, from a forced interpretation of the interrogation pronoun, which occurs in the refrain of each verse of the hymn. According to Ludwig, the meaning is : what other god than Prajāpati shall we worship. In general, 'Kasmai' means "To what god (we should offer our oblations. There is also one other meaning, we worship the Prajāpati, who is the form of happiness (Sukha). Another meaning is . We worship the Prajāpati whose name is "Ka". To my mind, here the meaning of "Kasmai" seems 'what is that' which amounts Anirvacanīya. It appears to be convincing after going through the whole hymn. Likewise "samavartata" has different meanings, It means 'born', as sāyana interprets and 'got embodied' as Ubbata comments, as said above. The hymn says : I that the Hiraṇyagrabha, who was in the beginning, was lord of all the beings. He fixed and holdeth up this earth and heaven what God shall we adore with our oblation ?

2. Giver of vital breath, of power and vigour, he whose commandments all the Gods acknowledge :

   The Lord of death, whose shade is life immortal. What God shall we adore with our oblation;

3. Who by his grandeur hath become Sole Ruler of all the moving would that breathes and slumbers;

   He who is Lord of men and Lord of cattle. What God shall be adore with our oblation;

4. His, through his might, are these snow—convered mountains, and men call sea and Rasā his possession :

   His arms are these, his are these heavenly regions. What God shall we adore with our oblation;

5. By him the heavens are strong and earth is stedfast, by him lights realm and sky vault are supported :

   By him the regions in mid air were measured. What God shall we adore with our oblation :

6. To him, supported by his help, two awrmies embattled look while trembling in their spirit,

   When over them the risen Sun is shining. What God shall we adore with our oblation ?

7. What time the mighty waters came, containing the universal germs, producing Agni,

   thence sprang the Gods one spirit into being. What God shall we adore with our oblation ?

8. He in his might surveyed the floods containing productive force nd generating worship.

   He is the God of gods, and none beside him. What God shall we adore with our oblation ?

9. Never may he harm us who is earth's Begetter, nor he whose laws are sure, the heavens' creator.

   He who brought forth the great and lucid waters. What God shall we adore with our oblation ?

10. Prajāpati ! thou only comprehendest all these created things, and none beside three.

    Grant us our hearts' desire when we invoke three : may we have store of riches in possession.

Carrying our the above mentioned purport, the Hiraṇya-garbha reads thus :—

हिरण्यगर्भः समवर्तताग्रे भूतस्य जातः पतिरेक आसीत् ।
स दाधार पृथिवीं द्यामुतेमां कस्मै देवाय हविषा विधेम ॥ 1

य आत्मदा बलदा यस्य विश्व उपासते प्रशिषं यस्य देवाः ।
यस्यच्छायामृतं यस्य मृत्युः कस्मै देवाय हविषा विधेम ॥ 2

यः प्राणतो निमिषतो महित्वैक इद्राजा जगतो बभूव ।
य ईशे अस्य द्विपदश्चतुष्पदः कस्मै देवाय हविषा विधेम ॥ 3

यस्य मे हिमवन्तो महित्वा यस्य समुद्रं रसया सहाहु ।
यस्येमाः प्रदिशो यस्य बाहू कस्मै देवाय हविषा विधेम ॥ 4

येन द्यौरुग्रा पृथिवी च दृळहा येन स्वः स्तभितं येन नाकः ।
यो अन्तरिक्ष रजसो विमान कस्मै देवाय हविषा विधेम ॥ 5

यं क्रन्दसी अवसा तस्तभाने अभ्यैक्षेतां मनसा रेजमाने ।
यत्रातिथि सूर उदितो विभाति कस्मै देवाय हविषा विधेम ॥ 6

आपो ह यद्बृहतीर्विश्वमायन्गर्भं दधाना जनयन्तीरग्निम् ।
ततो देवानां समवर्ततासुरेकः कस्मै देवाय हविषा विधेम ॥ 7

यश्चिदापो महिना पर्यपश्यद्दक्षं दधाना जनयन्तीर्यज्ञम् ।
या देवेष्वधि देव एक आसीत् कस्मै देवाय हविषा विधेम ॥ 8

मा नो हिंसीज्जनिता यः पृथिव्यायो वा दिवं सत्य धर्मा जजान ।
यश्चापश्चन्द्रा बृहतीर्जजान कस्मै देवाय हविषा विधेम ॥ 9

प्रजापते न त्वदेतान्यन्यो विश्वा जातानि परि ता बभूव ।
यत्कामास्ते जुहुमस्तन्नो अस्तु वयं स्याम पतयो रयीणाम् ॥ 10

The Viśvakarmā sūkta also is most important from the cosmogonic view-point. The deity Viśvakarmā is the father and procreator of all beings, though himself, he is uncreated. Viśvakarmā generated the primitive waters. To him, the Ṛgvedic sage says :

Who is our father, our creator, our maker,
Who every place doeth known and every creature,
By whom alone to gods their names were given,
To him all other creatures go to ask him[1]

The Ṛgveda further describes the Viśvakarmā as a creator as well as a controller. It says "what was the position, which and whence was the principle, from which the all seeing Viśvakarmā produced the earth and disclosed the sky by his might. The one god, who has one very side eyes, on every side a face, on every side, aıms, on every side, feet, when producing the skay and earth, shapes them with his arms and with his wings . . . Do thou Viśvakarmā, grant to they friends those thy abodes which are the highest, the largest and the middle—may a generous son remain here to us.[2] The following verses further prove the creatonship and Lordships of Viśvakarmā :

या ते धामानि परमाणि यावमा या मध्यमा विश्वकर्मन्नुतेमा ।
शिक्षा सखिभ्यो हविषि स्वधाव: स्वयं यजस्व तन्वं वृधान: ।।

ऋ० 10-91-5

विश्वकर्मन्हविषा वावृधान: स्वयं यजस्व पृथिवीमुत द्यां ।
मुह्य ं त्वन्ये अभितो जनास इहास्माकं मघवा सूरिरस्तु ।।

ऋ० 9-17-6

वाचस्पतिं विश्वकर्माणमूतये मनोजुवं वाजे अद्या हुवेम ।
स नो विश्वानि हवनानि जोषद्विश्वशंभूरवसे साधुकर्मा ।।

ऋ० 9-17-7

---

1. Ṛgveda, V.X. 82 (Kaegi's translation).
2. See Muir, Sanskrit Texts, Vol. IV, pp. 6 & 7.

विश्वकर्मा विमना आद्विहाया धाता विधाता परमोत संदृक् ।
तेषामिष्टानि समिषा मदंति यत्रा सप्तऋषीन्पर एकमाहुः ॥
ऋ० 10-92-2

विभ्राजञ्ज्योतिषा स्वरगच्छो रोचनं दिवः ।
येनेमा विश्वा भुवनान्याभृता विश्वकर्मणा विश्वदेव्यावता ।
ऋ० 10-171-4

त्वमिन्द्राभिभूरसि त्वं सूर्यमरीचयः ।
विश्वकर्मा विश्वदेवो महाँ असि ॥ ऋ० 6-5-1

In the RV, the văk hymn also represents the theory of cousation, wherein vāk, the daughter of the Ṛṣi Ambhṛṇī, has been described as satcidānanda Brahman, and thus the substratum of the whole universe. The same idea we find at another place in the Ṛgveda and it is—"vāgeva viśvā bhuvanāni jajñye". What śayana says vāk, the daughter of Ambhṛṇī fully knew the Brahma-vidyā. As Peterson says, vāk is speach personified, the world, the first creation and representative of spirit, and the means of communication between man and God".[1]

The vāk says that—

1. I travel with the Rudras and the Vasus, with the Ādityas and All Gods I wanter.

   I hold aloft both Varuṇa and Mitra, Indra and Agni, and the Pair of Aśvins.

2. I cherish and sustain high swelling Soma, and Tvaṣṭā I support, Pūṣan, and Bhaga. I load with wealth the zealous sacrificer who pours the juice and offers his oblation.

3. I am the Queen, the gatherer up of treasures, most thoughtful, first of those who merit worship. Thus

---

1. Peterson, The Hymns of the Ṛgveda p. 571, F.N.

Gods have established me in many places with many homes to enter and abide in.

4. Through me alone all eat the food that feeds them, —each man who sees, breathes, hears the word outspoken. They know it not, but yet they dwell beside me. Hear, one and all, the truth as I declare it.

5. I, verily, myself announce and utter the work that Gods and men alike shall welcome. I make the man I love exceeding mighty, make him a sage, and a Brāhmaṇa.

6. I bend the bow for Rudra that his arrow may strike and slay the hater of devotion. I rouse and roder battle for the people, and I have penetrated Earth and Heaven.

7. On the world's summit I bring forth the Father : my home is in the water, the ocean. Thence I extend over all existing creatures, and touch even younder heaven with my forehead.

8. I breathe a strong breath like the wind and tempest, the while I hold together all existence.

Beyond this wide earth and behond the heavens I have become so mighty in my grandeur.

According to the vāk hymn, vāk-Brahman is interpreted as the substratum of the whole world. This idea can be said as the seed—form of the śabda—Brahmavāda of Bhartṛhari. In Bhartṛhari's philosophy, the objective world is vivarta[1] of śābda and this idea has been developed in the tenet—form of the philosophy of word and meaning. In seventh verse of the vāk hymn, the idea regarding väk as Brahman, the creator is

1. Anâdinidhanam Brahma śabda-tattvam yadakṣaram. Vivartate' ! thabhāvena Prakṛyā jagator yatḥa. Vākyapadīya, 1.1.

clear. The following comments of Peterson, explaining the meaning of the word 'Pitaram' in the seventh verse, also support the above view : "The Father Heaven or Sky, produced from vāk identified with Paramātmā, the supreme and universal soul". The following views of Wallis on cosmology confirm the vāk as the creator of the world. Wallis observes thus; 'Vāc 'Speech' is celebrated alone in two whole hymns, X. 71, and X. 125, of which the former shows that the primary application of the name was to the voice of the hymn, the means of communication between heaven and earth at the sacrifice. The other hymns illustrate the constant assimilation of the varied phenomena of nature to the sacrifice; all that has a voice in nature, the thunder of the storm, the reawaking of life at dawn, with songs of rejoicing over the new birth of the world, are embodied in this Vāc in the same way as it is said of Bṛhaspati, that he embraces all things that are. It is thus another expression for that idea of the unity of the world, which we have seen crowning the mystical speculations of all the more abstract hymns of the collection'.[1]

The Vāk hymn is as follows :

अहम् रुद्रेभिर्वसुभिश्चराम्यहमादित्यैरुत विश्वदेवैः ।
अहम् मित्रावरुणोभा बिभर्म्यहमिन्द्राग्नी अहमश्विनोभा ॥ 1

अहं सोममाहनसं विभर्म्यहं त्वष्टारमुत पूषणं भगम् ।
अहं दधामि द्रविणं हविष्मते सुप्राव्ये यजमानाय सुन्वते ॥ 2

अहं राष्ट्री संगमनी वसूनां चिकितुषी प्रथमा यज्ञियानाम् ।
तां मा देवा व्यदधुः पुरुत्रा भूरिस्थात्रां भूर्यावेशयन्तीम् ॥ 3

मया सो अन्नमत्ति यो विपश्यति यः प्राणिति य ईं शृणोत्युक्तम् ।
अमन्तवो मां त उपं क्षियन्ति श्रुधि श्रुत श्रद्धिव ते वदामि ॥ 4

1. Cosmology of the Ṛgveda p. 85. See, also Weber, Vac and Aoyoc, indiche Studies, IX. 473-480; and Max Muller, The Vedānta-Philosophy, 144-147.

अहमेव स्वयमिदं वदामि जुष्टं देवेभिरुत मानुषेभिः ।
यं कामये तं तमुग्रं कृणोमि तं ब्रह्माणं तमृषिं तं सुमेधाम् ॥ 5

अहं रुद्राय धनुरातनोमि ब्रह्मद्विषे शरवे हन्तवा उ ।
अहं जनाय समदं कृणोम्यहं द्यावापृथिवी आ विवेश ॥ 6

अहं सुवे पितरमस्य मूर्धन्मम योनिरप्स्वन्तः समुद्रे ।
ततो वि तिष्ठे भुवनानु विश्वोतामूं द्यां वर्ष्मणोप स्पृशामि ॥ 7

अहमेव वात इव प्र वाम्यारभमाणा भुवनानि विश्वा ।
परो दिवा पर एना पृथिव्यैतावती महिना सं बभूव ॥ 8

From the cosmogonic view point, Bṛhaspati hymn also is worth considering. Bṛhaspati has been mentioned as the creator Brahma and also the Lord of Brahma, the creator and that is why he is also called Brahmaṇaspati.

The Bṛhaspati is addressed in eleven entire hymns, and in two others conjointly with Indra. He is also, but less frequently, called Brahmaṇaspati, 'Lord of Prayer; the doublets alternating in the same hymn. His physical features are few; he is sharp-horned and blue-backed; golden coloured and ruddy. He is armed with bow and arrows, and wields a golden hatchet or an iron axe. He has a car drawn by ruddy steeds, which slays the goblins bursts open the cow stalls and wins the light Called the father of the gods, he is also said to have blown forth their births like a blacksmith, like Agni, he is both a domestic and a Brāhman priest, he is the generator of all prayers and without him sacrifice does not succeed. His song goes to heaven, and he is associated with singers. In several passages he is identified with Agni, from whom, however, he is much oftener distinguished. He is often invoked with Indra some of whose epithets, such as maghavan bountiful and vajrin wielder of the bolkt he shares. He has thus been drawn into the Indra myth of the release of the cows. Accompanied by his singing host he rends Vala with a roar and drives out the cows. In so doing he dispels the darkness and finds the light. As regards his relation to his worshippers, he is said to help and protect the pious man, to prolong life, and to remove disease.

Bṛhaspati is a purely Indian deity. The double accent and the parallel and name Brahmaṇaspati indicate that the first member is the genitive of a noun "bṛh" from the same root as brahman, and that the name thus means Lord of Prayer'.

He seems originally to have represented an aspect of Agni, as a divine priest, presiding over devotion, an aspect which had already attained as independent character by the beginning of the Ṛgvedic period. As the divine brāhmaṇa priest he seems to have been the prototype of Brahmā, the chief of the later Hindu triad.

The hymn reads thus :

1. Yas tastambha sahasā vi jmo antān
Bṛhaspatis triṣad-hastho raveṇa,
tam pratnāsa ṛsāyo didhiānaḥ
puro viprā dadhire mandrajihvam

2. dhunoayah supraketam madanto
Bṛhaspate, abhiye nas tatasre
prsantam sṛpram adabdham ūrvam;
Bṛhaspate, rakṣatād asya yonim

3. Brhaspate, yā paramā parāvad,
ata ā ta ṛtaspṛśo ni ṣeduḥ.
tubhyam khātā avatā adridugdhā
madhvaḥ ścotanti abhito virapśam.

4. Bhaspatiḥ prathamam jāyamāno
maho jyotiṣaḥ, parame vioman,
saptāsyas-tuvijāto raveṇa
vi saptaraśmir adhamat tamāṃsi.

5. eva pitre viśvadevāya vṛṣṇe
yajñairvidhema, namasā, havirbhiḥ,
Bṛhaspate, supraja vīravanto
vayamsiạma pạtayo rayīṇām.

6. sa id rājā pratijanyāni viśvā
śuṣmeṇa tasthāv-abhi vīrieṇa,
Brhaspatim yaḥ subhṛtam bibharti,
valgūyati, vandate pūrvabhājam

7. sa it kṣeti sudhita okasi sve,
tasma ila pinvate viśvadānīm;
tasmai viśaḥ svayam-evā namante,
yasmin brahmā rājani pūrva eti.

8. apratīto jayati sam dhanāni
pratijanyāni uta yā sajanyā,
avasyave yo varivaḥkṛṇoti
brahmaṇe rājā, tam avanti devāḥ.

9. indraś ca somam pibatam, Bṛahaspate,
asmin yajñe mandasānā vṛṣaṇvasū;
ā vam viśantu indavah suā bhuvo;
a same rayim sarvavīramniyachatam.

10. Bhas; ata, Indra, vardhatām naḥ;
sacā sa vām sumatir bhūtu asme,
āviṣṭam dhiyo; jigṛtam puramdhīr;
jajastamaryo vanuṣām arātīḥ.

11. sa suṣṭubhā, sa rkvata gaṇena
valam ruroja phaligam raveṇa
Bṛhaspatir usriyā havyasūdaḥ
Kanikradad-vāvaśatīr ud ājat.

Thus summing up we find the following views on cosmogony, in the Ṛgveda :

1. Because of this universe is some subtle reality, which is described Sat in Ṛgveda. It is also described as Asat and different from Sat and Asat both as the Nāsadīya Sūkta says.

2. The Nāsadīya sūkta further mentions the "Tapas" as the cause of creation and this "Tapas" is saṁkalpa.

3. As the Hiraṇyagarbha Sūkta mentions, the Hiraṇyagarbha is the base of all devine light and it is the great power of the Universe from which all other powers and existences divine and earthly are derived. This idea is a nearest approach to the later idea of Brahman, which was described as the cause of all creation, in the Upaniṣads, the Brahmasūtra and the śāṁkarabhāṣya. The vāk, the power of speech also has been mentioned at the base of all the world. This view is fully developed in the form of śabda-Brahma concept in 7th century A.D. 5. Bṛhaspati is Brahmā, the creator or the Lord of Brahmā, Brahmaṇaspati. This view recognises Bṛhaspati, as the creator.

First of all, it may be impressed upon that the above views are not contradictory and out of them, the second and third view which mention "Tapas" and "Hiraṇyagarbha" as the cause of creation, are quite scientific. The other views mentioned above can be said theoritical, but not unscientific.

It may also be added that the Ṛgvedic cosmogony has two aspects mainly : (i) the mythological and (i) the philosophical. The mythological aspect has two currents. The one regards the universe as the result of mechanical production, the work of carpenters and joiner's skill; the other represents it as the result of natural generation.[1] In the Ṛgveda there is a querry "what was the wood and what was the tree out of which they built heaven and earth.[2] In this regard the Taittirīya Brāhmaṇa says that "Brahman is the wood and Brahman the tree from which the heaven and earth were made".[3] The heaven and earth are some times spoken of as universal parents and parentage is sometimes attributed to Aditi and Dakṣa. As far as the philosophical aspect of the Ṛgvedic cosmogony is concerned, the Puruṣa sūkta attracts our immediate attention. As has been earlier said the Puruṣa is

1. See, Macdonell, Vedic Mythology, p. 11.
2. Ṛgveda, X. 81.4.
3. Taittirīya Brāhmaṇa, 2.8.9.6.

the whole universe. There are also hymns in the RV which call the Sun as soul (Ātman) of all, the movable and immovable.[1] The concept of cosmogony described in the Nāsadīya sūkta, the Hiraṇyagarbha sūkta and the vāk sukta as discussed earlier, was prominantly considered within the purview of Philosophical aspect of cosmogony.

The Yajurvedic view

The sacrifical descriptions are the main contents of the Yajurveda. Nevertheless there are found some views on cosmogony directely and indirectly. In 31st chapter of the Yajurveda, the sacrificial puruṣa has been mentioned as the cause of universal creation and the puruṣa has been described as the highest principle in the Yajurveda. Like the Ṛgveda, in Yajurveda too, the Puruṣa has been understood as the highest of all and the all-pervading, as mentioned above in the treatment of puruṣa in the Ṛgveda. It is also noteworthy that Prajāpati, Puruṣa and Brahman are the same, according to the Yajurveda.[2]

The Atharva Veda and the Cosmogony

The Cosmogonic views are also prevalant in the Atharvaveda. In Atharvaveda Kāla has been mentioned as the cause of the cosmos. "Kāle tapaḥ Kāle jyeṣtham kāle Brahma samāhitam. Kāloha sarvasyeśvaroyaḥ pitāsit Prājāpateḥ" (A.V. 19. 53.8).

In Atharvaveda (19.54) also kāla has been indicated as the creator of various objects. The Kāla as the source of creation is like that of Ṛta, which is the eternal principle of the whole world order. The logic of similarity between Ṛta and Kāla is, that both are moving and that Ṛta is from the root "ṛ" (to go). Therefore the deities are described as born and increased by Ṛta. (Ṛtajāta, Ṛtavṛddha.)[3] According to

1. RV. 1.115.
2. See, Yajurveda chapter 32.
3. See, J.N. Shende, The Religion & Philosophy of the Atharvaveda p. 218, BORI, Poona 1952.

the AV. Brahman is identified with kāla[1] and thus all things are circumscribed by the kāla. Therefore the power behind the whole universe is the eternal time or the Brahman, as the AVs. Accordingly all seers, worlds and creatures are in Kāla (AV. 19.53.10). Also Āṅgiras and Atharvan, the creators are in kāla. The Kāla[2] is the substratum.

The Atharvaveda describes Brahman as the crude form. Accordingly, first the Brahman is born and then the highest vena, manifested himself from the horizen[3] Brahman, the first born, highest principle resides in the mid air. It animates all plants. It does not reside on the earth or in the heaven. It is the water in the mid air and its forms are on the earth.[4] Born between earth and heaven, it prevaded its seat in the heaven and on earth. It made firm the great rodasī. The seer says that the favour of Atharvan on Bṛhaspati the relation of the gods, is competent to make any one the creator of all, a poet and a god.[5] The seer speaks of the special charm as possessed of the immortal and unharmful spirit and as manifesting its womb.[6] This miraculous power of the charm attained the ordinances and displayed wonderful forms. It entered its own origin and understood the unspoken speech. From this spirit flowed forth the gold, which assumed immortal names. It may be the origin point of the Hiraṇya-garbha, which is the cause of universal creation. From the view-point of cosmogony, it is interesting to note that the Ātharvaṇic seers thought of many deities, endowed with the qualities of the creator and of highest creator. The Atharvaved further says that the seers conceived of gods, who guard before directions and who agree among themselves to

1. A.V. 19.53.9.
2. A.V. 19.54.5.
3. A.V. 4.1.1.
4. A.V. 13.2.1-3.
5. A.V. 4.1.7.
6. A.V. 5.1.1.

promote the order of the universe.[1] But Prajāpati is said to be superior to all these gods. Prajāpati is born of the Ṛta and Kala.[2] Thus Prajāpati, who creates all creatures is also born of eternal world order and time. According to the Atharvaveda procreation is the main function of Prajāpati.

Taking in view the detailed cosmogonic theory, the Atharvaveda says that Ātman in man is the most distinguished manifestation of Brahman and the man is the special creation of Brahman. Describing about the creation of the parts and particles of the body, the AV says that the Brahman fashioned the hair, bones, limbs, sinews, joints and flash of man. It put together its thighs, feet, knee joints, head, hands, face, ribs, nipples, sides, tongue and neck and enveloped all them in skin.[3] Afterwards, the particular complexion was brought in. After this, the gods entered in the human body and then the sleep, weariness, distress, sin, oldage and baldness entered in the body. The AV further says that the theft, illdoing, wrong, truth, sacrifice, glory, strength, vigour, prosperity and adversity, generosity and thrift, hunger and thrust, consure and praise, faith, sacrificial gift, knowledge and ignorance, Ṛcs, Sāmans, Yajus, Brahman, joy, enjoyment, laughter, sport, dance and talk and prattles entered the body. After the feelings and tendencies entered body, the senses such as the eye, ear, speech and mind and breaths such as prāṇa, Apāna, samāna, Udāna, and vyāna entered the body. The AV further says that afterwards, the fluid elements in the body, in the blood and bladder, the secret, clear, thick and scanty was made to settle down in the body and then the seminal fluid was fashioned. In this manner, all limbs, flesh blood, bones, breaths, senses, feelings, thoughts, emotions, volitions and seminal fluids were fashioned and arranged in their respective places in the body

1. A.V. 11.61.22.
2. A.V. 131.61, 19.53.10.
3. A.V. 11.18.12-16.

of the man and then the Brahman entered in it. The body of man is the stronghold of Brahman, covered with immortality.[1] By the above mentioned cosmogonic analysis, it may be interpreted the Brahman is the substractum (Adhiṣṭhāna) of the whole physique and the physical creation, like senses and the body is the resting place of all physical and mental formations

The Brahmanic stand point

It may be said at the outset that in the Brāhmaṇas, the cosmogonic view generally requires the agency of a creator, who is not always, the beginning point like the 'Sat' of the Ṛgveda and it may also be mentioned that in the Brāhmaṇas, the theory of evolution is mixed with the theory of creation, it is therefore that the Prajapati is sometimes mentioned as the creator and at other places the creator is described to have floated in the primeval water as the cosmic golden egg, the Hiraṇyagarbha. According to the Śatapatha Brāhmaṇa, it may be said that the concept of Brahman had acquired a great significance as the supreme principle of cosmogonic view. The Śatapatha says that in the beginning this universe was the Brahman. It created the gods and having created the gods, it made them ascend these worlds : Agni this (terrestrial) world, Vāyu the air, and Sūrya the sky...and then the Brahman it selfwent up to the spherebeyond it considered 'How can I descend again into these worlds'. It then descended again by means of form and name. These are the great forces of Brahman.[2] At an other place, Brahman has been described as the ultimate being in the universe and is identified with Prajāpati, Puruṣa and Prāṇa.[3] At another place Brahman is said as s ayumbhū (self born), who performs

1. I.A.V. 11.8.28, 10.2.26-29.
2. See, Eggling's Tr. of Śatapatha Brāhmaṇa, S.B.E. Vol. XLIX, pp. 27, 28.
3. See, S.B.E XL. III pp. 59, 60, 400 & XLIV p. 409.

austerities and who offered his ownself in the creatures and the creatures in his own self, and thus compassed supremacy over the creatures.[1] This concept of Brahman did not come to the mind of German Scholars, Haug & Roth. For Haug, Brahman meant, (i) food, food offering (ii) The chant of sāma-singer (iii) magical formula (iv) duly completed ceremonies (v) the chant and sacrificial gift (vi) The recitation of the hotṛ and (vii) great. To Roth it also means "the devotion which manifests itself as longing and satisfaction of the soul and reachesforth to the gods. This idea is also found in the Puruṣa Sūkta, wherein Puruṣa pervdes the world with only a fourth part of Himself, whereas the remaining three parts transcend to a region beyond. The Puruṣa is atonce the part, present and future.[2] This view is most significant from the cosmogonic point.

The Upanisadic cosmogony

While taking into account, the cosmogonic views in the Upaniṣads, it is interesting to note that the prominent idea of Viśvakarman & Hiraṇyagarbha is not found in the Upaniṣads, in the sense, it is found in the Ṛgveda the terms are found in the śvetāśvataropaniṣad. The use of Brahmaṇaspati is found no where in the Upaniṣads. To me, it seems that in the Upaniṣads, all these and such other concepts have been merged in the concept of Brahman or Ātman. To a great extent, it is reasonable and convincing for avoiding the confusion of so appearing the various discrepant concepts of creation. Thus, the Upaniṣads advocate Brahman as the substratum of the whole world & with its Power Māyā it becomes the cause of the worldly creation.[3] Further more, the Ātman has been mentioned as the cause of Ākāśa and from Akāśa Vāyu, from Vāyu, Agni, from Agni, Āpaḥ from Āpaḥ (water), earth was evoluted. Therefore it is because of

1. See S.B.E. Vol. XL. IX, p. 418.
2. Ṛgveda, 10.90.
3. Yato Vā imāni bhūtāni Jāyante, Taitti. Upa. 3.1.1.

Māyā that Brahman is the efficient cause of the world, while Māyā is the constitutent cause. It was therefrom that the sūkṣamaśarīra as well as the gross elements were evoluted. In this regard, the Chāndogyopaniṣad also mentions about the theory of Trivitkaraṇa[1] which explains the process of mixing the subtle elements (Tanmātrās) for the purpose of elemental formation. The theory of quintuplication (Pañcīkaraṇa) is also a development in the same direction. The Taittirīyopaniṣad (3.1.1.) also indicates the dissolution (Pralaya) of the world in Brahman.[2] Thus it is true to say that the cosmogonic ideas found in the older Upaniṣads are accurate and systematic and it is quite natural for they are fully elaborated thoughts based on the Jñānakāṇḍa of the Samhitās.

---

1. Tāsām trivṛtam ekaikam karvāṇi iti seyam devatemāstisro devatā anenaiva jivenātmana anu praviśya nāmarūpevyākarot Ch. Upa. 6.3.30.
2. Yat prayanti abhisamviśanti ca. Taitti, Upaniṣad 3.1.1.

The Veda and Vedānta

The Vedas are the oldest and chief reservoir of knowledge, which contain in themselves various facets of learning like spiritual, philosophical, empirical, devine, mythological, scientific, natural, social, cultural and so on. They are the revelations of the Ṛṣis and have come to us through the Śravaṇa tradition and it is therefore that their category is Śruti. It would be appropriate to say that the later Purāṇic, Philosophic, religious and cultural knowledge is an elaboration and enunciation of the basic knowledge prevalent in the Vedas. The contents of the Vedas are mainly related to Karma-kāṇḍa and the Jñānakāṇḍa. Accordingly the later two—philosophical systems, the Pūrvamīmāṃsā and the Vedānta, are the most prominent philosophical outcome of the Vedas. So to say of the Uttaramīmāṃsā or the Vedānta, it is the finality of the Vedic thought, as the term, Vedānta is itself indicative (Veda + A-anta). Here in 'anta' means Siddhānta, a final concept. Now, therefore it is evident that the Vedāntic thoughts richly contained in the Upaniṣads and reasonably and authoritatively propounded by Gauḍapāda and Śaṅkara, are deeprooted in the philosophical texts of the Vedas, specially the Ṛgveda-Samhitā In the Ṛgveda, the Nasadīya Sūkta (X. 129), the Hiraṇyagarbha-sūkta (X. 121.), the Puruṣasūkta (X 190), the Vis-vakarmāś-ūkta (R.V. X. 91), the Vāksūkta (X. 125), and the Bṛhaspati-sūkta are clearly supportive of the later Advaitic concept. These hints have already been explained earlier. Besides, the idea of one reality (R.V. 1.164.46), a mention of unborn (Ajanmā) (R.V. 10.164.6) which according to Sāyaṇa's view, is the basic of the later concept of Brahman and the description of Haṃsa as Paramātman in the Ṛgveda[1] further supports the later Advaitic theory of Vedānta. Here the Haṃsa has been described as Āditya, who is Brahman and none else. The Aitareya Brāhmaṇa also mentions about Haṃsa, who is Āditya.[2]

The above mentioned Ṛgvedic hints clearly support the view that they have the seed like views of later upaniṣadic and Śaṅkarite Vedānta in them and it is accordingly and appropriately that Śaṅkarācārya enunciates his Advaitic concept as an elaboration of the Vedic thought. Apart from the Ṛgveda, the Yajurveda, the Sāmaveda and the Atharva veda also found a clear base for later Vedāntic view. In the Yajurveda, Paramātman has been given many names like Indra, Mitra, Varuṇa, Agni, Divya, Suparṇa, Garutmān Yama and Matariś-vā. He has also been called as Agni, Āditya, Vāyu, Candramā, Śukra, Brahma, Āp-a and Prajapati. It has also been said that Paramātman is all-pervading and the substratum of all.[3] The Yajurveda also says that Paramātman is the Lord of all the Bhūtas and the Adhiṣṭhāna of all the Lokas.[4] The Sāma Veda also plays in the same tune. As Griffith also says : "The Sāmaveda or the Veda of holy songs, third in the usual order of enumeration of the three Vedas, ranks next in sanctity and litergical importance to the Ṛgveda or Veda of recited praise.[5] The Gītā also signifies its importance to mention "Vedānām Sāmavedossms."[6] In the Sāmaveda, Brahman, the supreme truth

1. R.V. 4.4.5.
2. Haṃsaḥśuciṣadityeṣa vai haṃsa śuciṣat. Aitareya brāhmaṇa, 4.20.
3. Yajurveda, 32, 1-5.
4. Yo bhūtānamadhipatiryasmin lokāḥ adhiṣritāḥ Y.V. 20.30.
5. R.T.H. Griffith, The Hymns of the Sāmaveda, Pref. 1226. Bana.
6. Bhagawadgītā, 10.22.

has been described as truth.[1] At another place, in the Sāmaveda Brahman (not naming it) has been indicated as the cause of the Universe.[2] The word 'tat' herein (S.V. 6.3.17), as Sāyana finds, means Brahman. The commentator Stevenson understands by it the original cause of the universe, that primoval cause alone.[3] To my mind, Stevenson is quite correct to explain, Tat' as the cause of the Universe, which was later described as Brahman, in Vedāntic thought. Further more in the Sāma Veda, there is also a mention of Brahma jñāna or Brahmānanda.[4] In this manner, the Sāmaveda also clearly presents the seed-ideas of later Advaita Vedānta. Likewise, the contents of Atharvaveda also oftenly support the Vedāntic view of philosophy. For example, the Atharva Veda indicates that Brahman exists in the hearts of all. (A.V. 20.1) (20.1.1.1.). Commenting on it, Sāyaṇa says that Brahman is the substratum and the world is superimposed on it and therefore there is nondulity, between the two.[5] Explaining the Vedāntic view of reality, the Atharvaveda mentions that Brahman through the Māyā Ś-akti takes the form of Āditya and pervades the whole world with its Tejas.[6] Describing further the all pervading character of Brahman, the Atharva Veda says that Brahmā, Śiva, Hari, Indra and Akṣara, all are Brahman.[7] As it is admitted in Vedānta, the

---

1. Sāmveda, 6, 3, 4, 10
2. Tadihāsa bhuvaneşu jyeşṭham, Sāmaveda, 6.3.17.
3. Griffith, The Hymns of the Sāmaveda, p. 206, Footnote.
4. Sāmveda, IX, 2.10.
5. Yatra yasmin adhiṣṭhānarūpe
   Brahmaṇi Visvam aropitam,
   Kṛtsnam Jagat eka-rūpam ekākāram bhavati,
   āropitasya adhiṣṭhāna-Vyatirekeṇa
   Sattvābhāvāt. Sāyaṇabhāṣya. 2.1.1.10.
6. See, Sāyaṇa bhāṣya, A.V.S. 4.1.1.1.
7. See, Sāyaṇabhāṣya, A.V.S. 7.1.1.1.

Atharvaveda also mentions that Māyā is an obstacle in the Sākṣātkāra of Virāṭ puruṣa.[1]

Thus, it is evident, by the above analysis, that the Saṃhitās, contain the basic threads of the later Vedāntic thought in one way or the other, but it is to be admitted that the Vedic Vedānta views are not there in a formal and doctrinal manner. It is because the Vedic expressions are the freelance revelations of the Ṛṣis and not the formal doctrines as they are found today Moreover like the Saṃhitās, the Brāhmaṇas and the Āraṇyakas also indicate the Vedāntic ideas. The Śatapatha Brāhmaṇa which has a epitomic status, contains clear out views on philosophy, particularly the Vedānta. It describes that in the beginning, there was Brahman only[2] and it created the gods first, like Agni, Vāyu and Sūrya and made them the Lord of Martya loka, Vāyu loka and Ākāśa loka, respectively.[3] Afterwards, Brahman appeared in name of form. Brahman—has also been said as S-vayambhūḥ in the Śatapatha Brāhmaṇa.[4] Mentioning about the creative process, the Śatapathabrāhmaṇa says that in the beginning, there was neither Sat nor Asat and it was mind only, which desired to be many. This is a popular idea of the Upaniṣads, which is mentioned in the Taittirīyopaniṣad,[5] as earlier also discussed, analysing the Vedic cosmogony. There is also the mention of Īśvara in the Śatapatha-brāhmaṇa, and it is there in the sense of highly competent entity.[6] The Aitareyabrāhmaṇa mentions Brahman, as Bṛhaspati.[7] Also Brahman has been described as Virāt, in

1. See, Sāyaṇabhāṣya, 8. V. 9.9.
2 Śatapathabrāhmaṇa, 11.2.3.1.
3. Śata. brāh. 11.2.3.1. Hariswami's comm.
4. S.B.E. Vol. XLIV, pp. 417, 418.
5. Taittiriyopaniṣad, Brahmavallī, 6.
6. See, Śatapathabrāhmaṇa, 13 2.9 6, 13.1.2.4 & 13.3.4.
7. Aitareya brāhmaṇa, 3.2.13.

in the Aitareya brāhmaṇa.[1] In the Taittiriya brāhmaṇa, Brahman has been said as the wood and tree (cause of the Dyūloka and the Bhūloka.[2] There, in the Taittirīya-brāhmaṇa, the word Brahma-Vādin has been used in the sense of Brahma-Vettā.[3] Also the word Brahmavid occurs in the Taittirīya-brāhmaṇa.[4] The Pañcaviṃśa-Brāhmaṇa also makes a mention of the Brahma-Vādin.[5] It may also be pointed out that in the D-aivata-brāhmaṇa of the Sāmaveda, Brahman has been described as the basic cause of all the Sāmans.[6] The Āraṇyakas also contain the views related to Vedānta. The Aitareyāraṇyaka mentions Parama-puruṣa as Prajāpati.[7] It further says that Ātman is all pervading.[8] According to the Aitareyāraṇyaka, the Satcidānanda-Paramātman is the creation of the Universe and it was only who existed in the very beginning of the creation.[9] In the Aitareyāraṇyaka, Brahman has also been described as Prajñāna and it has been expounded that Karman and Brahman, both are the means of Mokṣa.[10] In the taittirīyāraṇyaka, describing the all pervading characteristic of Brahman,

1. Aitareya-brāhmaṇa, I Part, p. 28, Ānandāśrama, Varanasi.
2. Brahma vauam Brahma-sa vṛkṣa āsīt, yato dyāvā pṛthivi niṣṭa taksuḥ. Taitti. Brāhmaṇa, 2.8.9.6.
3. Brahma-Vādino vadanti. Taitti. brāhmaṇa, 1.3.10.6.
4. Taittirīya brāhmaṇa, 1.4.8.6.
5. Pañeaviṃśabrāhmaṇa, 4.3.3., 6.4.15.
6. D-aivata brāhmaṇa, 2.21 & See, Sayaṇa-bhāṣya on it.
7. Aitareyāraṇy-aka, 2.1.2.
8. Yāvati-vai dyāvā pṛthivī tāvānātmā. Aitareyāraṇyaka, 1.3.8.
9. See—Dr. Mangal Dev Shastri, Aitareyāraṇyaka-paryālocanam, p. 35.
10. Eṣa panthāḥ —etat Karma, etad Brahma, Ibid, 2.1.1.

it has been said that Agni, Vāyu, Sūrya, Candramā, Śukra, water and the Prajapati, all are Brahman.[1] Likewise it is also mentioned that Brahmā, Siva, Hari, Indra, Akṣara and the ultimate reality is Brahman. One of the prominent view explained in the later Vedānta is that who knows Brahman, becomes Brahman ("Brahma vid Brahmaira-bhavati"). The same view is prevalent in the Tattirīyāraṇyaka (2.1). The Taittirīyāraṇyaka also presents the view that after creating the universe, Paramātman entered in it.[2] So also the Sānkhāyanā which has been called by Cowele as Kauṣītakyāraṇyaka, which has been called by Cowele as Kauṣītakyā-raṇyaka, says that Ātman is Brahman and Brahman is Apūrva, Apara, Anapara, Ananta and Abahya.[3]

The above analysis of the Saṃ-hitās, the Brāhmaṇas, and the Āraṇyakas, regarding the finding of the Vedāntic threads in them clearly evinces the fact that the Vedic vāṅmaya founds the basic idea of one reality, which is the substratum of the whole universe. The same has been described differently in the Vedas, as some times Sat, sometimes Asat, some times different from Sat and Asat and thus Anirvacanīya, sometimes Puruṣa, Hiraṇyagarbha, Ṛta, tapas and Satya and so on. It is therefore that the Muṇḍaka says that the Vedānta exists in the Veda like the oil exists in Tila corn.[4] The Śrīmadbhāgavata also mentions that Brahman & Ātman is the subject of the Vedas : Vedāḥ hyātma Visayāḥ Srimad-bhāgavata, 11.21.35. Searching the philosophical ideas in the Ṛgveda, Keith also says : "The earliest poetry of India

---

1. Tadevāgnistadvāyustatsūryastaccandramaḥ tadeva Śukram tad Brahma, tat āpaḥ tat Prajāpat ḥ, Taittirīyāraṇyaka, 10-1-2.
2. Taittirīyāraṇyaka, 8.6.
3. See, Sāṅkhāyanaraṇyaka, Chapter xiii, Ānaṇḍāṣrama, 1922.
4. Tileṣu-tailamiva veḍe veḍāntaḥ supratiṣṭhitaḥ. Muṇḍ. Upa. 1.9.

already contains many traces of the essential character of the philosophy of India.[1]

Now it may be examined that how far the Vedic seeds of Vedānta are fruited in the Upaniṣads, the fountain head of Indian philosophy and later in the Vedānta philosophy of Gauḍapāda and Śaṅkara. This will justify a co-relation between Veda and Vedānta, on one hand and the historical development of the Advaita Vedānta on the other.

For finding the Vedāntic elaboration in the Upaniṣads, let us first start with the concept of Brahman, the essence of Vedānta philosophy. The concept of the Saṃhitās has been doctrinized as Brahman in Upaniṣadic philosophy, it may be said at the outset. The crux of Upaniṣadic philosophy is to establish Brahman as non-dual reality and as a substratum on which the whole world is superimposed. The Chāndogyopaniṣad advocates that there is nothing beyond Brahman. It says that as after having the knowledge of a piece of gold, the whole gold is known, after the knowledge of a blade of steel, all the objects made of steel are known and after the knowledge of a piece of clay, all the objects made of clay are known, the same way, after knowing Brahman everything is known.[2] This upaniṣadic explanation supports the view that the world is the Vivarta of Brahman and therefore there is non-duality in Brahman and the world,[3] as the water and its waves are non-dual. According to the Upaniṣads, the names and forms apparent in the world are not real and they are mere appearance. Have the Upaniṣads teach about the non-difference in various casts and the reality of Ātman, may be witnessed in the Bṛhadāraṇyaka Upaniṣad, when it says that the Brahmanhood, Kṣatriyahood, all the Lokas, all the gods,

---

1. Keith, Religion and Philosophy of the Veda, 433 (Harvard Oriental series, Longman Vol. 32).
2. See ch. Upa. 6.1.2-7.
3. Br Upa. 4.2.6.

and all the Bhūtās, are the same Ātman. Explaining the characteristics of Brahman, the Taittirīyopaniṣad says that it is Brahman from whom all the Bhūtās are created, in whom subsisted and in the end, dissolved.[1] Describing non-duality between Brahman and the world, in an anological manner, the Kaṭhopaniṣad (6.1) mentions that the world-tree is rooted in Brahman. It says that Brahman is like the ancient fig tree (Asvattha), which has its root above and the branches below. The Gītā also says likewise (Ūrdhvamūlamadhaḥ śākhamaś-rattham prāhuravyayam, chandāṇsi if any a parṇaṁ yastaṃ veda savedavit B.G. 15.1). It is pure and immortal and in it, all the worlds rest and no one ever goes beyond it. As Radha Krishnan says this description has its analogue in the description of the tree Igdrasil in Scandinavian mythology.[2] The Bhagawadgītā also uses this analogy and illustration and teaches to cut off the tree of existence by the potent weapon of nonattachment (Aśvatthamenaṃ mvirudhamī lamārainga-śastrena B.G. XV. 3). The Śvetāśvatara (III. 9) and the Maitrī Upaniṣad (vi. 4) also, use the illustration of the Aśvattha tree. In the Bṛhadāraṇyak Upaniṣad, Brahman has been described as Mūrtta and Amūrtta, Martya and Amartya and Sat and Asat both.[3] It has also been explained as Sat, Cit and Ānanda in the Bṛhadāraṇyakopaniṣad.[4] As the Chāndogyopaniṣad says, Brahman itself and its knowledge is supreme bliss.[5] Describing Brahman as imperishable and

---

1. Yato vā imāni bhūtāni Jayante, yata prayanti abhisaṃ-viśanti ca, tadvij j-nasasva tad Brahma. Taithi. Upa, 2.3.1.

2. Radhakrishnan, The Principal Upaniṣads, p. 641.

3. Dve vā Brahmaṇo rūpe Mūrttañca, Amūrttañca martyañca amartyañca sthitañca sacca tyacca. Bṛhadāraṇyakopaniṣad, 2.3.1.

4. Bṛ. Upa. 2.4.12.

5. Ch. Upa 7.23.2. Bṛ. Upa. 3.8.8.

denying it a substance or the possesser of attributes, the Bṛhadāraṇyakopaniṣad says that it is neither gross nor fine, neither short nor long, neither glowing red (like fire) and nor adhesive (like water). Brahman is neither shadow nor darkness and neither air nor space. It is unattached, without taste, without smell, without eyes, without ears, without voice, without mind, without radiance, without breath, without a mouth, without measure and having no within and without. It eats nothing and no one eats it. This is Yājñavalkya's teaching to Gārgī. Accordingly, it is beyond space and also beyond Time (Kāla), as the Śvetāśvataropaniṣad mentions.[1] The Bṛhadāraṇyaka Upaniṣad further says that Brahman is Akṣara[2] and beyond cause and effect; it is ultimate and thus unknowable. Brahman is absolute truth and there is nothing apart from Brahman.[3] It explains the all pervading characteristic of Brahman.[4] Supporting this view, the Bṛhadāraṇyak-opaniṣad says that Ātman should only be realized, heard of, reflected on and meditated upon and if it is done, all is known.

The enunciation of Brahman as Para and Apara, is a most worthmentioning contribution of Upaniṣadic philosophy. The Maitrī Upaniṣad mentions Akṣara as Brahman and further the two types of Brahman, as Para and Apara[5] or the Nirguṇa and Saguṇa (higher and lower) Brahman. The Para-Brahman is supreme and allpervading and thus the Bṛhadāra-

1. Parastṅkalāt. Śveta. Upa. 6.5.
2. See, Bṛ. Upa. 3.8.8, 9 & 10.
3. Na tu tad dvitiyamasti tatomyad-vibhaktam if at paśyas. Bṛ Upa. 4.3.23.
4. Ātmā vā are draṣṭavyaḥ, śrostavyo, mantavyo nididhyāsitavyah, Maitreyi atmano vā are darśanena, sravaṇena, matyā vijñā-nena idam sarvam viditam. Bṛ. Upa. 2.4.5.
5. Evaṃ hi āhaitat vai Satya-Kāma parancāparañca Brahma yad aum eyetad akṣaramiti. Maitrī, Upa. 6.5.

ṇyaka mentions it as Apūrva and Anapara.[1] The Śvetāśvatara also mentions of the Para Brahman.[2] and so also the Mukti Upaniṣad mentions the same.[3] The Praśnopaniṣad also says that the Auṅkāra is Para and Apara and it is through this knowledge that the wise man attains the one or the other.[4]

The Para Brahman of the Upaniṣads is indeterminate and the absolute while the Apara (determinate) is creator[5] and the controller (Niyntā) of the Universe. He is the Antaryāmin,[6] the inner controller, from within, who controls this world, the next world and every thing. Also the Māṇḍūkyopaniṣad says, that he is the Lord of all, knower of all, the inner controller, the source of all and he is the beginning and the end[7] of beings.[8] The Apara Brahman of the Upaniṣads is called Īśvara and he has Māyā as his Śakti.[9] It is because of Māyā that he is Upādānakāraṇa of the world and in his own capacity, he is the Nimittakāraṇa.

---

1. Tadetat Brahmā-pūrvamanapram. Bṛ. Upa. 2.5.19.
2. Tataḥ param Brahma bṛhantam. Ś-vet. Upa. 3.7.
3. Para-brahmāvadhūtam, Mukti Upa. 1.37.
4. Parancāparañca Brahma yad auṅkāraḥ, tasmāt vidvānetenaivā yatanena ikatatamanveti. Praśna Upa. 5.2.
5. Taitti. Upa. 3.1.
6. Ya imam lokam paraṁ ca lokam sarvāṇi ca bhūtāni yo' ntaro yamayatīti. Bṛ. Upa. 3.7.1 and see also Bṛ. Upa. 4.4.22.
7. Eṣa sarves varsah, eṣa sarvajñaḥ, eṣontaryāmī, eṣa yoniḥ sarvasya prabhavāpyayau hi bhūtānam. Māṇḍukyopaniṣad, 6.
8. Māyāntu prakṛtim vidyān māyinam tu maheśvaram. Ś-vet. Upa. 1.4.3.
9. Māyāntu prakṛtim vidyān māyinam tu maheśvaram. Svet. Upa. 1.4.3.

In Upaniṣadic philosophy, Ātman and Brahman are the same.[1] Ātman with his adjunct of Avidyā or Māyā is called Jīva, the individual soul and it is the Jīva who is the doer, the experineer of good and bad, that who is in bondage and who is liberated. Thus the whole phenomenality is related to Jīva.

Being the Śakti of Īśvara and adjunct of Jīva, Māyā plays a very significant role in the philosophical system of Vedānta. The world also is Māyā in Vedānta. As has been said above, it is because of Māyā that God is the creator of the universe. The Māyā may not be prevalent in the form of a composite doctrine in the Upaniṣads, but the idea of Māyā is very much there in the Upaniṣads. It occurs two times in the principal Upaniṣads; once in the Praśnopaniṣad (1.16), and once in the Bṛhadāraṇyakopaniṣad (2.5.19). In the Praśnopaniṣad, the word Māyā has been used for trikery or Mithyācāra.[2] According to Radhakrishnan, this has led to the view that the world is deceptive in character. This view is not contradictory to the later Vedāntic view of Māyā, according to which the world is not real, although it appears as such. It also indicates the deceptive character of the false world. The use of the word Māyā in the Bṛhadāraṇyaka (the Ṛgvedic expression)[3] is in the sense of a mysterious power. In the Śvetāśvatara also, the term Māyā occurs and it is there in the sense of Prakṛti,[4] which is the Śakti of Īśvara, according to Śaṅkara.[5] Also in other Upaniṣads, like the Kaivalyopaniṣad (1.12) and the Nṛsimhapūrvatāpinupaniṣad (3.1) the word Māyā occurs.[6] However Śaṅkara on the Upaniṣadic

1. Ayamātmā Brahma.
2. Teṣāmasau virājo Brahmaloko na yeṣu jihmam, anṛtam, na Māyā ceti. Praśna Upa. 1.16.
3. Indro mayabhiḥ pururūpaiyat. Bṛ. Upa. 2.5.19.
4. Śvetā, Upa. 1.4.3.
5. Iśvarasya Māyā—Śaktiḥ prakṛtih. Sāṅkara bhāṣya, 1.4.3.
6. See, Ram Murti Sharma, Advaita Vedānta, p. 115.

base, has expounded the doctrine of Māyā, supportive to his Advaita philosophy as well as the concept of phenomenal reality.

In Vedānta, the mission of an enquirer is liberation (Mokṣa) and it is the realization of self. Therefore according to the Vedāntic view, a person who realizes Brahman becomes Brahman. Thus the Muṇḍaka Upaniṣad says that he, who knows Brahman, crosses over sorrow and sins liberated from the knots of the secret place (of the heart) he becomes immortal.[1] It may be admi tted that there is no very clear distinction between Jīvanmukti and Vedahamukti in the Upaniṣads, as it is in later Vedanta, even then the Chāndogyopaniṣad and the Bṛhadāraṇy akopaniṣad clearly indicate the concept of Jīvanmukti. The Chāndogyopaniṣad says that as water does not cling to the leaf of lotus likewise evil does not cling to one, who knows Brahman.[2] So also the Bṛhadāraṇyakopaniṣad says that as the slough of a snake lies on an ant-hill, dead, cast off, even so lies this body and this disembodied immortal life is Brahman only.[3] Both these examples clarify the standpoint of Jīvanmukti, according to which one can become a Jīvanmukta, in this very life, after having realized Ātman or Brahman. The Muṇḍaka also says that after the realization of Pāramātman, the knot of Avidyā is cut and all doubts are dispelled and the Karmans are destructed (Muṇḍ. 2.2.9). As far as the Videhamukti is concerned, the Kaṭhopaniṣad says that the liberated leaves this body also in the end and he never takes rebirth. This is

1. Se yo ha vai tat paramam brahma veda brahmaiva bhavati, vāsyā brahmavit kule bhavati, tarati śokam tarati pāpmānam guhā-granthibhyo vimukto, mṛto bhavati. Muṇḍakopaniṣad, 3.2 9.
2. Yathā puṣkara palāśapo na śliṣyante, evam evamvidi pāpam karma na śliṣyata iti. Chā. Upa., 4.14.3.
3. Yathā hinirlvayanī vālmīke mṛtā pratyastā Śayīta evam eva idam Śarīram Śete. Bṛ. Upa. 4.7.7.

the state of Videhamukti.[1] The Videhamukta has no reason to take rebirth.[2]

Thus it is clear that the Vedāntic threads which are prevalent in the Samhitās, Brāhmaṇas and Āraṇyakas, are found expanded in the Upaniṣads. Also there are some ṛṣis and Ācāryas, like Bādari and Bodhāyana whose views on Vedānta are found closely or remotely and elaborated. But even in the Upaniṣads, the doctrinization and enunciation is not visible and this job was done mainly by Śaṅkarācārya and prior to him by Gauḍapādācarya. Now it is nccessary to take into account this aspect.

Gauḍapāda and Śaṅkara

In the field of Vedānta, the contribution of Gauḍapāda and Śaṅkara is epitomic. Even before them, thick and thin vedāntic reflections can be seen in the Brahmasūtra, the Purāṇas, the Bhagawadgītā, the tantra literature and the Yogavāśiṣṭha. But correct representative of the Upaniṣadic Vedānta, prior to Śaṅkara is Gauḍapāda, who (700 AD) enunciated the doctrine of Advaita, on the basis of his concept of unborn (Ajāti). Thus his main concept is known as Ajātavāda. According to Ajātavāda, the world in reality, is unborn and thus Māyā only. As Gauḍapāda propounds, it is an account of Māyā that the Jīva is not able to realize Brahman, and as soon as the Māye ignorance is away, the Jīva becomes competent to know the Advaitic reality, Brahman.[3] For the knower of reality the experiences of the waking state are just like a dream. As the experiences of the dream state are proved in the waking slate false, so the wordly experiences of the waking state are false in the state of

1. Vimuktaśca vimucyate. Kaṭha Upa. 5.1.
2. Dehād vimue eya mānasya Kimatra pariśiṣyate. Kaṭh. 5.4.
3. Anādi māyayā supto yadā Jivaḥ prabudhyate.
Ajamanidrama svapnama-dvaitam budhyate tadā. G.K. 1.36.

turīyā,[1] the state of Brahman. It is the state of non-duality.[2] In this state of Paramārtha, there is neither bondage nor liberation and nor there is a quest for liberation.[3]

The Śaṅkarite Advaita

Gauḍapādācārya explained his Advaitavāda doctrine in the Gauḍapādakārikā, the treatise which has a Buddhistic influence and it was quite obvious. Saṅkarācārya, the Prasiṣya of Gauḍapāda and disciple of Gobinda the ga atpāda fully expounded the doctrine of Advaita on the basis of the Vedic views and the Upaniṣadic philosophy, prominently. His Advaitavāda is also called as Brahmavāda or Brahmādvaitavāda. Śaṅkarācārya is a realist as well as an idealist. Accordingly Brahman is reality and it is the ideal to be achieved. In the Vedānta of Saṅkara, even the world is not entirely unreal and it has its phenomenally real status. Even the entirely unreal object has been categorised by Saṅkarācārya, to say it illusory (Prātibhāṣika). While Brahman is the Pāramārṭhika reality, the world is phenomenally real and the silver superimposed on conch shell or the snake superimposed on rope, is the example of illusory reality. Thus Saṅkarācārya has propounded the doctrine of Advaitic reality, keeping in view the pros and cons thereof. The Ācārya expounded his Advaitic tenet with the help of Adhiṣṭhāṇa and Adhyāsa concept. Accordingly Brahman is the substratum and the world is superimposed on it. Without admitting Brahman as Adhiṣṭhāna, the existential state of the world can not be proved. Not only this, even the mirage, which is illusory, can not be proved without admitting its base, the sand.[4]

1. G.K. 2.4.
2. Jñāte dvaitam na vidyate, G.K. 1.18.
3. Na nirodhona tpatlir na baddhona ca sādhakah. Na mumuksur na vai mukta ityesā paramārthatā. G.K. 2.62.
4. Nahi mṛga tṛṣṇi Kādayo, pi nirāspadā bhavanti. S.B.G. 13.14.

The Brahman of Advaitin, is although nameless and formless, it is a positive entity and thus it is not like the Śūnya of the Mādhyamika Buddhist. In this regard, Śaṅkara says that Brahman which is a permanent reality and non-dual appears to be Asat for dullards.[1] Śaṅkara also propounds Brahman as the cause of the origin, subsistance and dissolution of the world. He says : "Asya Jagato nāmarūpābhyām Vyākṛtasya aneka-Kartṛbhoktṛi saṃyuktasya pratiniyatadeśakālanimitta-Kṛyā phalāsrayasya—manasāpi acintyaracanārūpsya janmasthiti-bhaṅgam yataḥ sarvajñāt sarvaśakteḥ Kāraṇād bhavati, tad Brahma.[2]

As indicated in the Upaniṣads, Śaṅkara also expounds the two states of Brahman, the Para and Apara.[3] The Para is Brahman and the Apara is determinate Brahman (Saguṇa Īśvara), who is to be worshipped. It is Īśvara, who is the creator of the universe, because of His Māyā Sakti, Śaṅkarācārya propounding his concept of Māyā says that it is different from Sat and Asat both and thus it is Anirvacanīya. Śaṅkarācārya does not discriminate between Avidya and Māya and according to him Avidyā is the c use of bondage. Not to realize Brahman as supreme reality is Avidyā which is the cause of duality and thus it is the cause of pleasure and pain. When this Avidyā is removed, Brahman is known and this state of Brahma jnāna is the state of Brahman and also

---

1. Digdeśaguṇagati phala bheda śūnyam hi paramārthasad Advayam Brahma mandabuddhīnāmasad iva pratibhāti. S.B. Ch. Upa. 8.1.1.
2. B. S. S. B. 1.1.2. See also—Vanmanasā titattvamapi Brahmaṇo nābhāvabhi-prāyenābhidhīyate. B S.S.B. 3.2.22.
3. Kim punaḥ param Brahma, Kimaparamiti, ucyate, yatrāvidyakṛtanāmarūpādiviśeṣā dasthūlādi—Śabdairbrahmopadiśyate tat param. Tadeva yatra nāmarūpādi Viśeṣeṇa Kenacid viśiṣṭamupāsanāyopadiśyate manomayaprāṇaśarīro bhārupaḥ (Ch. 3.14.2) ityādiśabdaistadaparam. B.S.S.B. 4.3.14.

the state of Mokṣa.[1] In this state, the liberated lives his life in a very decent manner. For him, there is no enemy or friend. His treatment is equal to all. (Samatvam yoga ucyate, B.G. 2.48). It is in a natural way, that his activities are for the good of others. It is evident by the behaviour of saints like Swāmi Rāma Krisṇa-Paramahaṃsa, Vivekānanda, Arvinda Ghoṣa and others. The liberated or the Brahmajñānin lives in this world till the end of enjoyment of his Prārabdha Karmans which is unavoidable. And this is called the state of Jīvanmukti. It may be mentioned that after the enjoyment of Prārabdha Karmans, the liberated leaves his body and he never takes rebirth. It is also clear here as said above that the Jīvanmukta lives all-ways for the sake of society and social welfare.

The state and place of Īśvara in Śāṅkara Vedānta, is highly significant. He is Antaryāmin, Niyantā (controller) and the bestower of the result of good and bad actions of a person and thus an unbiased judge. He is equal to all. He is just like a cloud which rains equal in all fields. But even on the equal treatment of Īśvara to all human kind, if there is found a different state of persons, it is because of their different deeds and not because of any bias of Īśvara or his undeugrace unkind treatment. It is like the different kind of harvest in different fields, which is due to various factors like different kind of seed, land and such other things which help in the growth of the harvest. It may also be added here that there is no contradiction in the concept of Īśvara and Karman in Vedānta, because a person reaps the result of his Karmans, as he sows. Thus Īśvara just partoms the fruits of the Karmams of human beings.

It is to be further mentioned that every person has to experience the fruits of his Karmans of not only this life, but also of the last life.

---

1. Brahmaivamuktyavasthā.

Regarding the creatorship of Īśvara, it may be obvious to question that for what reason, there is a quest in him for creating the universe, as he has no desire, being Āptakāma. It is true to an extent, but Śaṅkara says that the sṛṣṭi is the Līlā (svabhāva) of Īśvara[1] and thus there is no question of any desire in him, for creation.

By the above analytical approach towards Śaṅkarite Advaita, it is evidently clear that Śaṅkarācārya authentically expounded the doctrine of Advaita or Brahman primarily on the basis of the Upaniṣadic philosophy, mainly prevalent in the ten principal Upaniṣads. As also has been earlier said, the Upaniṣadic philosophy has its deeper roots in the Saṃhitās, mainly the Ṛgveda saṃhitā, the Brāhmaṇas and the Āraṇyakas and therefore it is quite appropriate to state that the doctrine of Advaita is entirely a Vedic doctrine, as mentioned at the outset. In this regard, Keith can be correctly quoted, when he says : "The earliest poetry of India already contains many traces of the essential character of the philosophy of India.'"[2]

---

1. B.S.S.B. 2.1.33.
2. Keith, Religion and Philosophy of the Veda, P.433, Longman, Vol. 32, Harvard Oriental Series.

Problems of Mukti in Śaṅkarite Advaita

At the outset it would be proper to mention that on the empirical as well as the spiritual level Mukti gives a sense of release from bondage and happiness. So far as Śaṅkarācārya and his Advaitic concept is concerned, Mukti means Brahmanhood,[1] release from worldly bondage, realization of Brahman or the state of supreme knowledge and the highest bliss. Therefore the characteristics of Brahman, sat cit and ānanda,[2] can be said as the characteristics of Mukti. Being so, the concept of Mukti enunciated by Śaṅkarācārya cannot be equated with the Nirvāṇa of the Buddhist which is based on the tenets of negativity and nonessentialness. However, it cannot be denied that namelessness and formlessness regarding Mukti and Nirvāṇa are parallel in both the systems of philosophy. It may further be added that the falsehood of world and the realisation of supreme bliss can be said as the basis of the concept of Mukti in Advaitic thought. Thus it would be very much reasonable to take into consideration these points and some others related to them.

As in Advaita philosophy, the world stands as false and because the falsehood has created many misapprehensions, its meaning is to be primarily taken in view. Accordingly it may be said that while taking into account Śaṅkarācārya's falsehood view, it is to be kept in mind that he never meant complete negativity of the world by the idea of falsehood. What Śaṅkarācārya understood by falsehood is that the

---

1. Brahmaiva muktyavasthā, B S.B. III 5.52.
2. Saccidānanda Lakṣaṇaḥ, Aparokṣānubhūti.

world of name and form is not real like Brahman and thus it is false from the view point of permanent reality. As such reality in Śaṅkarācārya means the uncontradicated state at all times i.e. past, present and future.[1] One more point can be observed here that the world also cannot be said as phenomenally real and this may look surprising to some scholars who stressingly propound two more categories of reality, the Vyāvahārika and the Prātibhāsika apart from the Pāramārthika, according to Śaṅkarācārya. Their's is a wrong notion, because if Śaṅkarācārya admits these categories of reality, how can he be proved as a non-dualist. In this regard, it may further be added that Śaṅkarācārya no where mentions Vyāvahārika sattā or the Prātibhāsika sattā as such. It is also to be looked into that how the liberated take the world, while materially the world does not finish for even the liberated. It is a fact that even in front of a liberated the material world exists as it is. As for as the Advaitic view is concerned, for the liberated, the duality of the world ends and not the world. A Bṛahmajñānin realises Brahman in every thing. (Sarvaṁ khalvidaṁ-Brahma). So the Advaitic concept of Śaṅkarācārya is called as Kevalādvaita. To prove it in entirety a prominent post Śaṅkara Advaitin Madhusūdana Saraswatī has also propounded the falsehood of falsehood.[3] He argues that if the falsehood of the world is admitted, there is a scope for duality, because to prove the falsehood of the world itself indirectly justifies the standing of the world. It is hence that Madhusūdana Saraswatī propounds the falsehood of falsehood to maintain that it is only one reality in Śaṅkara Advaita, from the view point of the liberated. To object that the falsehood of falsehood further makes a way for proving the reality of the world due to the plea that by nega-

1. Yadviṣayā buddhir na vyabhicarati tat sat. Śāṅkra-bhāṣya, Bhagawadgītā, II. 16.
2. Chāndogyopaniṣad. (Ch. Up.) III. 14.1.
3. Advaitasiddhi, I.

ting the falsehood of the world, as Madhusūdana does, the world can be taken obviously as real, is not proper. It is because his attempt to prove the falsehood of falsehood is in the line of Śaṅkarācārya to justify the only reality of the ultimate Brahman.

About the behavioural life of the Tattvajñānin or Jīvanmukta, his attitude towards the dual world is to be known. Taking it into deep consideration, a post-Śaṅkara Advaitin, Prakāśānanda, the authar of the Vedāntasiddhānta-muktāvalī, states his view in the doctrinal form of Dṛṣṭisṛṣṭivāda and maintains that creation (Sṛṣṭi) is based on perception (Dṛṣṭi).[1] To elaborate, according to him it can be said that the dual creation is seen because it is perceived. To me, it does not seem to be proper, because it is not the perception of the dual world, which proves the creation, but the ignorant viewing of duality, which creates the sense of dual creation (Sṛṣṭi). It can be further justified to say that the Tattvajñānin also perceives the dual world, but he never sees the creation as dual, as Gauḍapāda also says: "Jñāte dvaitaṁ na vidyate". Thus the world "dṛṣṭi" in Dṛṣṭisṛṣṭivāda, should be understood for viewing duality (dvaita dṛṣṭi) and not for Pratyakṣa as explained by Prakāśānanda. It may further be stressed that Pratyakṣa of the worldy objects cannot be said as the cause of dual appearance of creation for the reason that even the liberated perceives the dual world, but he realizes non-quality in duality like the elephant made of clay (mṛdgajabhānavad). As far as the perception of world objects is concerned, it is undisputed and to support it, the following verse of the Upadeśasāhasrī (XI-13) can be quoted :

Suṣuptavajjājrati yo na paśyati
dvayñca paśyannapti cādvayatvataḥ

Tathā ca kurvannapi niskṛiyaśca ya
Sa ātmaviṇnāya iṭiha niscaryaḥ

---

1. Vedāntasiddhāntamuktāvalī, 1.

In this verse, the expression "dvayānca paśyannapi cādvayatvataḥ" clearly mentions that the Ātmavit or liberated sees non-duality in duality. Now it is clear that for the liberated, there is nothing apart from Brahman and that he realises the non-dual Brahman everywhere in this world. Here it is to be argued that to see Brahman in everything does not mean that the world of name and form is Brahman, but that Brahman is the substratum and the world is superimposition. As in the example of Suktirajata, the Sūkti is substruatum and the Rajata is superimposition so, also in the case of Brahman and the world, Brahman is the substratum and the world is superimposition. Thus a liberated realises only the substratum (Adhiṣṭhāna) and nothing non-dual.

It needs no elaboration that Mukti or the Tattvajnāna is the finality of metaphysical state and that can be said the state of supreme bliss and infinity. In this state, there is neither egoistic feeling and nor a quest for worldly enjoyment. But if it is so how the state of the Mahāvākya, Ahaṁ Brahmasmi[1] (I am Brahman.) which indicates egotism can be justified and further how the infinite Brahman can be an object of I-sense (Ahmanubhava). To this, the Advaitin's answer is that the state of 'Ahaṁ Brahmāsmi' is the state of Adhyāsa and therefore the state of Vṛtti and not the state of Brahmajñāna, as it appears.

While we take in view the concept of Mukti; it amounts that the knowledge of Paramātman is the final state and in this, the knot of nescience is cut, all doubts are dispelled and his deeds get terminated, as the Muṇḍaka Upaniṣad says :

> Bhidyate hṛdayagranthiśchidyante sarvasaṃśayāḥ,
> Kṣīyante cāsya karmāṇi tasmin dṛṣṭe parāvare.[2]

To evaluate the above statement, it may be observed that even the Ātmajñānin has to keep his body for experiençing

1. Bṛhadāraṇyaka Upaniṣad, 1.4.10.
2. Muṇḍakopaniṣad, II. 2.9.

the result of his prārabdha karmans. But if it is so, why the Upaniṣad states "Karmāṇi kṣīyante" all the karmans are destroyed. No doubt, that the Sañcita and Sañcīyamāṇa karmanis are destroyed after the Paramātmajñāna. Regarding the destruction of the prārabdha karmans Śaṅkarācārya says that the two, Sañcita and Sañcīyamāṇā are destroyed, but not the prārabdha karmans (Asya vichinna saṃśayasya nivṛttāvidyasya yāni vijñāotpatteḥ prāk kṛtāni janmāntarecāp ravṛttaphalāni jñānotpattisahabhāvīni ca kṣīyante Karmāṇi, natvetaj janmārambhakāni, pravṛttaphalatvāt).[1] This explanation of the Ācārya further needs an elaboration, because if in the state of complete (Pūrṇa) and final knowledge, the destruction of all karmans is not justified then the state of pūrṇatā and finality of the eternal knowledge becomes confusing and meaningless. Therefore the expression "Karmāṇi kṣīyante" should be interpreted in the light of the idea that even the prārabdha karmans of the Jñānin are destroyed, because their Bījatva is finished and thus they have no potentiality of producing another karmans. This can be said as the burning of the karmabīja with the fire of supreme knowledge, according to the following verse of the Gītā :

"Jñānāgni sarvakarmāṇi bhasmasāt kurute tathā"[2]

Śaṅkarācārya also comments on the above to say "tasmāt samyagdarśanaṁ sarvakarmaṇaṁ nirbījatve kāraṇam."[3] At this point, the criticism that how the same commentator gives a different version at two places, the Muṇḍaka and the Gītā, is not worthwhile, because in the Muṇḍaka this statement is based on the prime idea that the experience of the prārabdha karmans is a must; but finally states that after the Paramātmjñāna, all the Karmans are destroyed and thus there remains no scope for any contradiction, which is in the fitness of the philosophy of karmans.

---

1. Śāṅkarabhāṣya, Muṇḍaka. Up. II. 2.9.
2. Bhagawadgītā, IV. 37.
3. Śāṅkarabhāṣya, Gītā, IV, 37.

The Concept of Akṣara

The Akṣara is highly a dominant vedic, specifically an Upaniṣadic concept, which again finds a most significant place in the religion and philosophy of India, particularly Vedānta. In Ṛgveda-Saṃhitā, it has been mentioned as the cause of the universe.[1] The Upaniṣads explain the Akṣara concept at length and they mainly take it for Brahman. In the Bṛhadāraṇyaka, Yājñavalkya says that Brahman is Akṣara.[2] Śaṅkara also says that Akṣara is Paramātman and not the letter (Varṇa)[3]. Describing the supremacy and all pervasiveness of Akṣara, the Bṛhadāraṇyaka further says that the Akṣara is unseen, but it is seer, is unheard, but is the listener, is unknown, but is the knower. Yājñavalkya says to Gārgī that by the imperishable, the space is woven like warp & woof.[4]

Thus Akṣara is the supreme self in the Upaniṣadic Vedānta. Thus in Vedānta, there are mainly three states of self. Self, with the limited adjuncts of the body and the organs, the products of the ignorance—desire and will is called the individual soul; when the self has the limiting adjunct of eternal knowledge and power, it is called Anaryāmin, Parameś-vara. The same self is absolute, pure, & alone (Kevala) and the imperishable (Akṣara)

---

1. Yadakṣarātsambhavatīha-viśvam. RV 1.164.39.
2. Etidvaitādakṣaram. Bṛ. Upa. 3.8.8.
3. Akṣaram Paramātmā evanāvarṇaḥ. B.S.S. B. 1.3.10 See also, Etasya vākṣarasya prasāsare Bṛh. Upa. 1.3.9.
4. Tadvā etad akṣaraṃ Gārgī adṛṣṭaṃ draṣṭṛ. Bṛ. Upa. 3.8.11.

supreme self. The Kaṭha also mentions Akṣara as Para-brahma.[1] Referring to the Ṛgveda, the Śvetāśvatara says that the Vedas are intended to realize the supreme self. But for those, who study them, without undergoing the inward discipline, they are not of much. It mentions, for him who does not know that indestinctible being of the Ṛgveda, where on in the highest heaven all the gods reside, of what avail is the Ṛgveda to him ? They, indeed who know that rest fulfilled.[2] The Śvetāśvatara also indicates to another aspect of the Akṣara & says that in Akṣara Brahman, there are hidden, the knowledge (Vidyā)[3] & ignorance (Avidyā). The Vidyā is eternal, the Avidyā is mortal. He, who controls both, is Sākṣin.[4] The Maitrī Upaniṣad says that the Akṣara is pure and clean and it is wise, the ordainer, within all, shining, patient & tranquil.[5] Thus it is clear that the Upaniṣads mainly propound the Akṣara as Para-brahman[6] and it is said as the origin of the universe.[7] Giving a hint to Advaitic state of Akṣara—Brahman and the world, the Muṇḍaka says that as from the blazing fire sparks of like

---

1. Akṣaram Brahma yatparam. Kaṭha. 3.2.
2. Ṛco'kṣare parame vyoman yasmindevā adhi viś-ve niṣe duḥ, Yastam na Veda Kim ṛcā karisyati ya it tadvidus ta ime samāsate. Ibid, Śvet. Up. 4.8 , see also 1.7, 8, 10 and 4.18.
3. Dve akṣare brahma pare tuanante VidyāVidyenihite yatra gūdhe. Ksaram tvavidyā amṛtam, tu vidyā, vidyā-vidye Īśate yastu so'nyah. Śvet. 5.1.
4. Anya is ḥtat säkṣitvāt; S.B. Svet. 5.1.
5. Yaḥ prājño viḍharṇaḥ sarvāntaro'Kṣaraḥ śuddhaḥ pūtaḥ bhāntaḥ Īsāntaḥ. MaitrI. VII. 6.
6. Akṣarāt parataḥ paraḥ Muṇḍ. 2.1.2. Tadetat akṣaram brahma, Muṇḍ. 2.2.2. Akṣaram brahma sammitanm. Mahānā, 15.1.
7. Tathākṣarāt sambhavatīha Viś-vam, Muṇḍ. 1.1.7.

form issue forth by the thousands, the same way many kinds of beings issue forth from the immutable and they return thither to.[1]

The Praśna Upaniṣad explaining this state of Suṣupti describes Akṣara as the substratum (Adhiṣṭhāna) of the subject self and in this state, even the distinction of subject and object is not seen. The Praśna says that the subjective self is the seer, the toucher, the hearer, the smeller, the taster, the perceiver, the knower, the doer, the thinking self and the person. He becomes established in the supreme undecaying Self.[2] The Atharvaśīrṣopaniṣad mentions Akṣara as the origin of Kāla.[3] However all these Upaniṣads describe Akṣara as Brahman. But in the Chāndogyopaniṣad and some other Upaniṣads, the Akṣara has been described as Aum, prominently the sacred syllable.

Being the essence of the Upaniṣads (Sarvopaniṣadogāvah), obviously, the Gītā describes the Akṣara in more than one ways As it has been seen in the Upaniṣads, the Gītā also describes Akṣara as Brahman.[4] But in the Gītā, another picture of Akṣara is prevalant, according to which the Puruṣa has been mentioned as Kṣara & Akṣara both. Not

---

1. Tathākṣarāt dvividhā saumya bhāvāḥ prājāynte tatra caivāpi yanti. Muṇḍ. 2.1.10.
2. Eṣa hi draṣṭā, spraṣṭā, śrotā, ghrātā, rasayitā, mantā, boddhā, Kartā, Vijñānātmā Puruṣaḥ sa pare akṣar-ātmani sampratiṣṭhate. Praśna. II 9
3. Akṣarāt sanjāyate Kālaḥ. Atharvaśierṣopaniṣad 6.
1. Akṣaram Brahma paramam. B.G. 8.3
Yadakṣaram Vedavido Vadanti. B.G. 8.11
Avyaktol'Kṣara ucyate. B.G. 8.21
Tamakṣaram paramam-Veditavyam. B.G. 11.18 & also see B.G. 11.37, 12.1, 12.3.

only this, the Gītā also describes the Akṣara Puruṣa as Kūṭastha.[1]

Here, it is to be observed that if the Akṣara Puruṣa is Kūṭastha, the immutable, (Kūṭastho, kṣara ucyate, B.G. 15 18), then why Kṛṣṇa describes Himself as superior (Uttama) to Akṣara[2], which is Kūṭastha and as Kūṭastha it is the highest according to the Vedāntic view. To this, an answer is found in Śaṅkara who interprets Kūṭa as Māyā and thus the Kūṭastha as Māyāvin. He further says that the Kūṭastha, being the endless causal seed of the universe is said as Akṣara.[3] But Śaṅkara also understands Brahman or Paramātman mainly by Akṣara.

---

1. D-vā-vimau puruṣau loke Kṣaraṣcākṣara eva ca.
   Kṣaraḥ sarvāṇi bhūtāni kūṭastho'kṣara ucyate.
   B.G. 15.16.
2. Yasmāt Kṣaramatito' hamakṣarādapi cottamaḥ
   Ato'smi loke Vedeca prathitaḥ puruṣottamaḥ B.G. 15.18.
3. Kūto Māyā Vañcanā jihmatā kuṭiltā iti paryāyā anekā māyādi-prakāreṇa sthitāḥ kūṭasthāḥ saṃsāra-bījanantyād na Kṣarati iti Akṣara ucyate. S.B. B.G. 15.16,

Sankarācārya's relevance to the Present Age

It is curiously noteworthy that Śaṅkarācārya in his very short span of life propounded a philosophy, the philosophy of Advaita or the concept of one soul Theory on the basis of Upaniṣadic Thought, which became meaningful for the whole mankind, whether east or west and in all ages and circumstances. It is because of the same that in most parts of the world, there is seen a practical interest for its application and training, which is evident by the Vedāntic centres running through out the world. It can be further said that from the time of Vivekānanda's visit to America, during which the philosopher gave a new light to the Śaṅkarite thought, through his practical Vedānta, the Advaita of Śaṅkarācārya became more significant and popular in west. Also it should be admitted that Rādhā Krishnan's exposition of the Advaitic thought has further made it easy and approachable to the west as well as the English reader of the east. Obviously it makes one anxious to know the reasons because of which Śaṅkara's philosophy of Advaita has become so important and applicable to all, irrespective of cast of creed and in all times. To analyse it, first our attention goes to the concept of Ekātmavāda or Brahmavāda, the doctrine of Māyā, creation and liberation as well as the Vedāntic view of Adhikārin.

The Ekātmavāda concept which pleads the view of one soul in every human being, is the basic tenet which supports the idea of one mankind. It is this idea which interweaves the whole humanity in one thread and thus the draw-backs of present age like the ego of small and big, inferiority and superiority, cast and creed and the menace of violance is automatically remedied, if a person has a Vedāntic approach. As Śaṅkarārcāya advocates, the nature of Ātman or Brahman, which exists in every human being, is such that there remains no place for the distinction of Brāhmaṇa and Kṣatriya.[1] In his जन्माद्यस्ययत: bhāṣya, on the Upaniṣadic line, Śaṅkarācārya further proves Brahman as the source of creation of the whole mankind which indicates the universal character of his philosophy of Advaitism. The Ācārya, while propounding his philosophy of Advaita advocated the falsehood of the world, which means that the world is not permanently real, although it is real at the phenomenal level.[2] The Śaṅkarite idea of the falsehood of the world is an eye-opener for those who are very much devoted for the material gains neglecting the high human values based on Vedāntic spiritualism and humanism. Thus a person who lives following the Vedāntic human values based on the Vedāntic concept of reality, is never baffled or perturbed because of the material ups and downs. This way, the Vedānta can be of a great help for keeping the mind balanced, in this age of anxiety and anger. It may also be initiated here that as much as a person realises the inner reality of Ātman, he regains a self confidence and depth of intuition, due to spiritual energy which is the key to supreme happiness and ideal manhood. It is needless to say that self confidence and the intuitive experience is very much desirable in the present age of hollowness and superficiality.

The Vedāntic philosophy of Karman which pleads the unavoidability of experiencing the result of one's actions is further an indicator for those who never fear from doing bad actions in this age of corruption. Today's man does not care to foresee the result of his actions and blindly goes on to act bad deeds. This puts him to big trouble. What is entirely

1. Apetabrahmakṣatrādibhedam, B.S.S.B.I.I.I.
2. Satyānṛte mithunīkṛtya ahamidam mamedamiti naisargiko, yam lokavya-vahāraḥ, B.S.S.B. 1.1.1.

non-vedāntic, the feeling of undue attachment also is a cause of wrong doings. It can be of various types, like the attachment for wealth and our relatives and frinds as well as self purposes. In the present age, there is no need of searching the instances, in this regard, as the people are much interested in their own selfishness of money matter and false prestige and less in the performance of their duty and this evil of attachment and bondage can be said as the reason of modern day's many disasters like injustice in society and the official level. How Vedānta can help it, may be easily known through the Vedāntic view of liberation, which advocates the philosophy of detachment in action and not from action. As the Gītā says, no body can remain without performing actions[1] and not even a Jīvanmukta has to do some actions. Although in him, there is no interest either for good or bad actions. (शुभाशुभ परित्यागी) Thus it is in natural way that he always performs good actions. Therefore the attitude and state cf Mokṣa can be highly meaningful in present day's atmosphere of selfishness and hatred. Here this point can be stressed upon that Mokṣa does not mean always to leave this world, as there is also the state of Jīvanmukti, in which a person can do welfare of society without any selfish motive. In this connection, Rāma Krishṇa Paramahaṃsa, Vivekānanda, Rāma Tīrtha and Arvinda Ghosh may be quoted who devoted their life for the good and welfare of society. If a lesson of human service and practical Vedānta is taken from the above mentioned philosophers, the evils of modern age can be totally eradicated. Maharshi Ramaṇa, Annie Besant and Mother Teressa also can be included in the chain of modern Vedāntins, who have devoted themselves for human service and freedom of soul and society.

The qualifications of an Adhikārin of practical Vedānta as mentioned by Śaṅkarācārya are highly desirable in the

1. Nahi Kaścit kṣaṇamapi jātu tiṣṭhatyakarmakṛt B.G. III. 5.

present age of the environment of impatience, disquite and disturbance, dissatisfaction and intolerence as well as lack of faith in the scriptural teachings of the teacher. Mentioning the qualifications of the Adhikārin, the Bṛhadāraṇyaka Upaniṣad says that after having become quite subdued, satisfied, patient and collected (Samahita), a person realises self in self.[1]

No doubt, the above mentioned reference is general in its nature. But some of the Ācāryas of Advaita Philosophy, like Śaṁkarācārya, have taken in view the competence and qualifications of the Adhikārin, with proper attention and seriousness. In this regard, it will be desirable to say, that the question of Adhikārin has been treated in the Vedānta texts, like Vivekcūḍāmaṇi from the standpoint of learning the practical knowledge of the Vedānta-Śāstra and not from the view point of acquiring knowledge, Śaṁkarācārya, in his Upadeśasāhasrī, says, that the Vedānta is to be taught to one, who is of tranquil mind, who has subjugated his senses, who is free from faults, obedient to his teacher, endowed with virtues like discrimination, renunciation and forbearence etc. In his Vivekacūḍāmaṇi also Śaṁkarācārya has described the virtues of the Adhikārin in detail.

He says that the success depends essentially on a qualified aspirant (Adhikārin) and considering the qualifications of the Adhikārin of Ātmavidyā, he says that he should be intelligent, learned and skilled in arguing in favour of scriptures, and refuting counter arguments. He also mentions the four means of attaining the Ātmavidyā, i.e., discrimination between real and unreal, aversion to enjoyment of fruits of one's actions in this world and the upper world, the wealth or group of six attributes viz., calmness (Śama), self control (Dama), self withdrawl (Uparati), forbearance (Titikṣā)

1. Tasmādevamvit śānto dāntaḥ uparatastitikṣuḥ samāhito bhūtvā ātmanyevātmānam paśyati, Br. Upa. 4.4.23.

constant concentration on Brahman (Samādhāna), faith in the instructions of the scriptures and the Guru (Śraddhā) and the yearning for freedom, Mumukṣā.[1] Śaṁkarācārya says that calmness etc. can only be fruit-ful for person, who has an intense sense of renunciation and yearning for liberation.[2] Without renunciation and yearning for freedom, the śama etc. are merely for name, like water in a desert.[3] Thus it is quite clear that if a person has the qualifications of an Adhikārin, he can live an ideal life and achieve the best of happiness.

Furthermore Śaṅkarācārya's philosophy is relevent for removing the evil of castiesm and unequality. In his Ātmabodha, he clearly says that the creation of castes is based on Upādhi or Ajñāna and thus it is not real :

Nānopādhivaśādeva jātināmāśramādayaḥ. Ātmabodha. The Gītā also says that for whom the duality of difference does not exist and who have equal view for all, are engaged for the welfare of all.[4]

Although Śaṅkarācārya was a saṃnyāsin, for him, there was a great value of the house-holders. In this regard Mādhavācārya says that whatever is necessary, is the purity

---

1. Ādau nityānitya vastuvivekaḥ pariganyate. Ihāmutra phalabhogavirāgastadanantaram. Śamādiṣaṭkasampattir mumukṣatvamiti sphuṭam, V.C. 19.

2. Vairāgyaṁca mumukṣatvam tīvram yasya tu vidyate, tasminnevārthavantaḥsyuḥ phalavantaḥ kśamādayaḥ, V.C. 30.

3. *Ibid.*

4. Chinnadvaidhā yatātmānaḥ-sarvabhūta hite ratāḥ, B.G.V. 25.

of mind. It is immaterial whether one is a Saṃnyāsin or house-holder :

Mano Viśuddho gṛhī bhavet vāpyuta maskarī vā.

—Śaṅkaradigvijaya

To some, the Vedānta may be the subject of upper world, but it is not appropriate. Sarvajñātmamuni, in his Saṁkśepaśārīraka says that in this very life, the experience of Vedāntic great sentence like Aham Brahmāsmi is possible :

Atraiva Janmanibhavedapavargadāyi vākyaprasūtamanubhūtiphalāvasānam. Saṁkṣepaśārīraka, III. 339.

Thus it becomes clear that the Vedānta is very much meaningful for allsided progress of mankind and national integration and today's world of narrowness and hatred based on castiesm and the menace of communalism. The culture imbibed in Vedāntic concept of Ekātmavāda has the remedial measures which can uproot the social evils of the day. As indicated earlier, the Vedāntic culture based on the non-dual philosophical tenet of the Advaitins has a capability of uniting the whole man-kind in one thread, the way of "Vasudhaiva Kuṭumbakam". It teaches the lesson of "live and let live others" and advocates a Dharma, which does not come in the way of the followers of other Dharmas. It is because of this that the Vedāntic idea of soul has influenced the inventors and followers of Buddhism, Jainism, Mohammadism, Sikkhism, and so on. It may further be mentioned that saints like Nānaka and Kabīr were highly influenced by the Vedāntic thought.

Now it can be summed up that Śaṅkarācārya's Vedāntic view does not have simply a balming effect on the tense and disturbed mind of present age, but it also presents the fundamentals of ideal manhood and human behaviour alongwith a direction to reach the best aim of human life. As has been said earlier, the Vedāntic view is not only competent to solve the national problems; it has also been helpful in tackling the international issues through the philosophy of global co-operation. So also, the concept of common wealth, the United Nations, the policy of non-alignment and the Saarc have the one soul tenet of Vedānta in their back-ground kno wingly or unknowingly.

Therefore, Vedānta can be said as the best way for tackling the individual, social, religious, spiritual, national & international problems of the day and fostering world peace.

Citsukhācārya on Brahman and Avidyā

It needs no elaboration that 'Brahman' is an important element in Advaita philosophy and thus there is no Advaitin who has not shed sufficient light on the tenet of Brahman. It is thus that Citsukhācārya—the author of Abhiprāya-Prakāśikā has dealt with the concept in detail. It may be mentioned that the Abhiprāya-Prakāśikā is a commentary by Citsukha on the Brahmasiddhi of Ācār ya Maṇḍana Miśra. At the outset, it may be hinted that although, on the tenet of Brahman, quite sufficient literature by Advaitins is available, the author of Abhiprāya-Prakāśikā has taken in view quite a many significant points which are a great contribution to the Advaitic learning.

While taking note of the significance of Brahman, the supreme reality in Advaita Vedānta, it is warranted to mention that albiet Brahman is the highest reality in Advaita philosophy and thus its top priority is certain, Avidyā or Māyā also has got a very prominent place in the Advaitic network, because of its pivot role in enunciating the position of the tenet of Brahman. That is why the Upaniṣads, and the Vedāntins like Śaṅkarācārya and his posteriors have given due consideration to the doctrine of Māyā. Thus in very clear terms, it is needless to say that it may not be possible to propound the tenet of Brahman or Advaita without admitting the doctrine of Māyā. This is the main factor in mentioning of the doctrine of Māyā as the main thesis of Śaṅkarācārya, the fore-most Advaitin. Furthermore, in other words, it will not be too much to say that the doctrine of Avidyā or Māyā is more significant even than the tenet of Brahman, because it is the former which greatly helps the enunciation of the tenet of Brahman. It is with this view that the study of Avidyā is to be linked with the study of Brahman herein.

It is quite reasonable to say that the Upaniṣadic thoughts present a clear and broad back-ground for the latter Vedāntic philosophy. For example, it may not be too much to say that the tenet of Brahman initiated and explained by Vyāsa in his Brahma-Sūtra and Śaṅkarācārya in his Bhāṣyas is entirely based on the upaniṣadic concept of Brahman. Among the essential and significant characteristics of Brahman, Bliss or Ānanda is most significant. Needless to say that this Ānanda which is the very nature of Brahman has been very well mentioned in the Upaniṣads.[1] On the same line, in the Brahma-Sūtras—"Athāto Brahmajijñāsa", and "Janmādyasya Yataḥ", the concept of Brahman is presented in nutshell. The same way, Maṇḍana Miśra in his Brahman-siddhi mentions Brahman as Ānanda Eka, Amṛta, Aja, Vijñāna, Akṣara, Asarva, Sarva, Abhyāsa and Prajāpati.[2] Here, Citsukhācārya initiates a discussion on the point and says that if there is a Jijnāsā or Pravṛtti for Brahman, then how an enquirer or Jijñāsu can achieve his final peace for a person who has a desire can never achieve the supreme piece.[3] Furthermore, regarding the objectivity of Brahman, there can be an objection that if Brahman is an object, in that case, the non-duality of Advaita is not possible. It is, because, the moment, subjectivity and objectivity is accepted, the idea of duality is created. So far as, in this connection,

---

1. Ānandaddhi Imāni Bhūtāni Jāyante; (*Taittirīyo.* 3.6.1), Eṣosya Paramānandaḥ (*Bṛhadā.* 4.3.32), Vijñānamānandam (*Bṛhadā.* 3.9.28).
2. Brahmasiddhi, Page 3.
3. Sa Śāntimāpnoti Na Kāmakāmī—BG.II.70

the remedial answer of Citsukhācārya is concerned, he first of all, refutes the philosophy of Vijñāna of the Buddhist and says that the Vijñāna itself is the nature of essence and not a separate entity, and thus not a Prameya. Thus, the Abhiprāya-Prakāśikā explains that 'Brahman' which is pure bliss is Cit also, and because of this, it is a self-illumined reality which illuminess the whole unreal.[1]

Thinking upon the blissful nature of Ānandasvabhāvatā of Brahman, it is obvious to think that the Ānanda according to the Advaitin is absence of pain (Duḥkhābhāva) or something else. The Abhiprāya-Prakāśikā's answer to this is that the Duḥkhābhāva is worldly pleasure (Laukika-Sukha) and so it is decidedly different from the Supreme Bliss. Citsukhācārya - the author of the Abhiprāya-Prakāśikā admits the Laukika-sukha as the part (Aṁśa) of Paramānanda—the Supreme bliss, and this he propounds on the basis of Śruti—"Etasyaivānandasya anyam bhūta-mātramupajīvanti". To object this, it is said that how there can be a part of the indeterminate and absolute Brahman. But refuting this objection, the Abhiprāya-Prakāśikā mentions that as the partless ether, due to the adjuncts of 'Ghaṭa' and Maṭha takes their shape, like-wise, it is the Paramānanda originally which takes the form of the worldly pleasure, because of the adjunct of Manas etc.[2]

It may be said that if Paramānanda is accepted as the eternal nature of Brahman, then, there will be a possibility of the state of Jīvanmukti always and thus there will remain no place for the state of world (Saṁsāra-daśā), there is no doubt about the permanent blissful nature of Ātman, but it is on account of Avidyā that the individual soul is not capable of realizing its own blissful nature. In this manner, till

1. See 'Abhiprāya-prakāśikā', Page-30.
2. "Ghaṭākāsavat tadupādhyavacchedāt" (Abhiprāya-prakāśikā P. 38).

the Avidyā is removed, there will be a full scope for Saṁsāra-daśā. But, after the removal of Avidyā, the blissful nature of Brahman will be realized and in that state there will only be the state of Brahman—the blissful Supreme reality.[1]

The author of the Abhiprāya-prakāśikā finds a difference between the Jīvanmukta and the Ajñānin on a different line on the basis of Śruti. He says that an ignorant sees a difference of name and form while the Jñānin Jīvanmukta understands the world like dual and not dual and thus in his eyes the world is non-dual.[2]

Citsukhācārya—the author of Abhiprāya-prakāśikā, mentions some Buddistic views regarding the state of Brahman and 'Mukti'. According to one Buddistic view, the state in which the inflictions created of vāsanās are destructed, is called the state of the attainment of Brahman. As the Abhiprāya-prakāśikā states, attainment of Brahman means Mukti.[3] According to the other view, after the destruction of the Vāsanās and objectivity when the pure knowledge is attained, it is called the state of attainment of Brahman. Really speaking, the above two Buddhistic views are not much different from the Vedāntic view of knowledge. Citsukhācārya further presenting the view-point of pūrvapakṣin, says that it is not proper to understand Brahma as an entity without beginning and end. If it is so accepted, then there will be nothing to gain or nothing to lose. Secondly, if it is understood that Brahman has knowledge as its nature, it is also not true. Because, the permanent knowledge will be neither cessable nor attainable. Furthermore, if it is said

---

1. See 'Abhiprāya-prakāśikā', P. 39.
2. Yadi tāttvikam bheda-darśanam tathā 'Nānā paśyati' ityeva ucyate na tu 'nāneva paśyati' iti. (Abhiprāya-prakāśikā, P. 43.
3. Brahmaprāptiśabdena cātra Muktirvivakṣyate, (Abhi. P. 53).

that Avidyā or Ajñāna is the nature of Brahman, it will also not be proper on the ground that because of the eternity of Brahman, Avidyā can never be removed. To my mind, the above mentioned objections never stand valid on logical grounds. First of all, it is not proper to say that if Brahman is accepted as without beginning and end, there will be nothing to lose and gain. To this, it can be said that because of Avidyā or ignorance the beginningless and endless Brahman is not realized. But the moment the real knowledge of Brahman is initiated, the highest objective of Mukti or Brahmajñāna is achieved as a matter of fact. So also, it may be mentioned that Brahman has knowledge or Vidyā as its nature ; but it is on account of Avidyā that the true nature of Brahman remains veiled and thus it is after attaining right knowledge Vidyā that the Avidyā is destructed.[1]

In fact Avidyā plays an important role in the realm of Advaita Philosophy. Citsukhācārya explains the special characteristic of Avidyā to mention it as Tattvā-grahaṇāt-mikā and the Vidyā as Tattvā-grahaṇātmikā which makes further clear that it is because of the former that 'Brahman or reality is not known and it is because of the latter —Vidyā that Brahman or the fact reality becomes subject of realization. Thus, it may be said that the treatment of Brahman is not new to the author of Abhiprāya-prakāśikā, Ācārya, Citsukha. He has dealt with this problem with most original and logical explanations and observations on the basis of the tenets propounded in the Brahmasiddhi of Maṇḍana Miśra and quite some other works of Vedāntins like the Bhāvaśuddhi of Ānandapūrṇa Muni. The above mentioned points are further found elaborated in the commentary[2] of Śaṅkha-pāṇi on Brahma-siddhi.

---

1. Vidyayā tasyāḥ bījaśakterdāhāt (Brahmasūtra-śāṅkara-bhāṣya 1.4.3).
2. The 'Bhāvasuddhi' of 'Ānandapūrṇa Muni' and the commentary of 'Śaṅkhapāṇi' has been published by Madras Government.

In this context of the treatment of Brahman, it is quite proper to say that philosophically the tenet of Brahman cannot be proved without taking into consideration, the concept of Avidyā or Māyā. It is thus that from Śaṅkarācārya, the great exponent of Advaita-Brahman till today there is not any Advaitin who has expounded the Advaita Brahman without taking the help of the doctrine of Māyā. To explain it, it can be said that Brahman as creator, controller and sustainer can only be justified if the superimposed relation between Brahman and Māyā is admitted. Briefly speaking, it may be mentioned that if Īsvara is Abhinnopādāna—Nimitta-Kāraṇa, it is because of his Śakti, Māyā. So also the creatorship of Brahman is only justified because of Māyā. It may also be emphasized here that Brahman with Māyā is defined as Īśvara in Śāṅkara Vedānta, and he is the creator of the whole universe. Thus, it makes clear that it is because of Avidyā or Māyā that Brahman gets activated for various activities like creation. Although, being entirely a knowledge or Jñāna it is totally actionless. Now, it becomes further clear that the actionless "Brahman" becomes full of activity on accouut of its power, Māyā. While admitting Avidyā as Śakti it is obvious to be curious for knowing the locus of Avidyā. Is Brahman the locus of Avidyā or Īśvara or Jīva ? It is said that Brahman which is self-effulgent and eternal knowledge cannot be locus of Avidyā. Because, Avidyā—the ignorance, and knowledge cannot exist together. Therefore, Maṇḍana Miśra in Brahmasiddhi admits Jīva as the locus of Avidyā.[1] Here, the question can be raised how the Jīva which is basically Brahman can be locus of Avidyā. To this, it can be answered that, no doubt, in the Advaita Vedānta Philosophy, Jīva in its true-nature is Brahman, but it is on account of the adjunct that the individual soul or Jīva is recognised as separate. But Citsukhācarya putting an

1. Yattu Kasyāvidyeti, Jīvānāmiti brāmaḥ (Brahmasiddhi, P. 10).

objection to the above mentioned explanation regarding the means of removal of Avidyā says that if the Śravaṇa, Manana and Nididhyāsana are Avidyā as said above, how they can remove the Avidyā, because the removal of Avidyā through Avidyā is never logical. Even if so granted, anyhow, then for the removal of śravaṇa etc., which are Avidyā, another Avidyā will be needed and this process will go on, which will be the state of no statement or endless series of statements (Anavasthā).[1] But putting counter argument to the above objection, the author of the Abhiprāya-prakāśikā says that the śravaṇa etc. are related to Paramārtha, Brahman, to an extent and therefore after removing the Avidyā of name and form they also do not stand, as they themselves also are the form of Avidyā, one way or the other.[2] Regarding the removal of śravana etc. after removing the Avidyā through them, an example is given by the Vedāntins that as after cleaning the muddy water, the Kataka powder also disappears, the same way, the śravaṇa etc. also do not stand after the removal of Avidyā. It is also in the same manner, that Avidyā being the adjunct, is the creator of jīvahood, but after the right knowledge of Brahman, the Avidyā also is removed. Describing the importance of Avidyā for attaining the state of eternity, another example given by the Vedāntins is that after taking the medicinal water the bad water in the stomach is cured. The same way, through the śravaṇa etc. the state of Avidyā of duality is removed and the final reality, Brahman is known. It is thus that the Īśopaniṣad mentions the importance of Vidyā and Avidyā both for the attainment of eternal state.[3]

---

1. Avidyātvepi avidyāntaranivartakatāyām svanivṛttayepi avidyantaramanveṣaṇīyam ityanavasthā (Abhi. Prā. P. 67).
2. Advaitaviṣayāḥ śravaṇādayo bhedadarśanavirodhino bhedamātram nivartayantaḥ tadaviśeṣāt śravaṇādilakṣaṇamapi bhedamnivartayanti (Abhi. P. 67).
3. Īśopa. 11.

Ānandapūrṇa Muni, the author of Bhāvaśuddhi commenting on the example of medicinal water says that the example is not proper, because it is the medicine which cures the bad water inside the stomach and not the water[1] as said above, while citing the example. In this context, the example given by Maṇḍana Miśra in his Brahmasiddhi seems justified when he says that as the poison can be cured with poison[2], so the Avidyā,[3] can be cured with Avidyā as mentioned in the Īśopaniṣad. Citsukhācārya making an original comment on the problem and proving the superiority of Avidyā to Brahma Vidyā says that it is Avidyā in the form of śravaṇa etc. through which a person gets over the mortality, because its (Avidyā's) object is Brahman, while Brahmavidyā is the mode of mind (Antaḥkaraṇa Vṛtti) having Brahman as its object.[4] The author of Abhiprāya-prakāśikā further proving the significance of Avidyā says that it is through the unreal lineal gavaya (Rekhā garaya) and the lines of the script that the real gavaya and the varṇas are known respectively. Accordingly it is through Avidyā.

Brahma vidyā is realized. The great Advaitin, Śaṅkarācārya also justifying the importance of false Avidyā says that even though the false nake bite, a man is found dying.[5] This

1. See Brahmasiddhi, Abhi. Pra. P. 13.
2. Yathā ca viṣam viṣāntaram śamayati svayam ca śāmyati, B.S. P. 13.
3. Atra Brahmavidyā Brahmasvarūpā, Viṣayāntaḥkaraṇa-Vṛttiḥ. Avidyā tu Śravaṇādilakṣaṇā, tayā vibhāgadarśanam mṛtum tarati, tasyā avidyātve, Brahmaviṣayatayā Balavattvāt (Abhi-Prā. P. 70).
4. Gavāyatmanā Varṇākārena ca asatvepi Svarūpeṇa tatra rekhā nāsatyā, ityarthaḥ, Na rekhāmātram gavayādipratipattihetuḥ, Kintu Viśiṣṭa gavavādytamakam. (Abhi. Pra. P. 71).
5. Śaṅkāviṣādinimittamaraṇādikāryopalabdheḥ, B.S.S.B. II 1.4.

way, the importance of Avidyā in attaining the final knowledge, the Brahma Vidyā is quite justify and it is the Brahmavidyā or Brahmajnāna which is described as Mokṣa, or Brahman, the final mission of an enquirer into Brahman, the Brahma jijañ su.

Finalising citsukha's comments on Brahman and Avidyā, the two basic and most prominent tenets of Advaitic thought, it may be summed up that the archaie vedāntins like Śaṅkarācārya, Sureśvara, Padmapādācārya, Vācaspatimiśra and many others had already made a serious and śāstric approach regarding the study of Brahman and Avidyā, but the most of the aspects and points raised by Citsukha in his Abhiprāyaprakāśikā were unheard and unexplored prior to him, as has been mentioned above. Apart from it, the dialectic of style of citsukha, evident in his Tattva-Prakāśikā and to a certain extent in the Abhiprāya-prakāśikā is highly impressive and śāstric although he borrowed it from Śrıharṣa, the author of Khaṇḍana Khaṇḍan Khādya.[1]

1. Brahmaiva hi muktyavasthā B.S.S.B. 3.4. 52.

Visṇu as Brahman in the Visṇupurāṇa

The origin of monistic as well as theistic approach can be evinced allaiet in its initial stage in the Ṛgvedic hymns like Bahudhā "*Ekam Sad viprābahudhā vadanti.*" Accordingly, the only reality has been described in many ways, like Viṣṇu, Śiva and Śakti and so on. While the reality is, one, basically and without name and form, it is without qualities and thus an absolute entity. The same Vedic thread of reality, has been very well elaborated in the principal Upaniṣads, in the form of the tenet of Brahman and has been further enunciated by Śaṅkarācārya, the Advaitin, commenting on the Prasthānatrayī. particularly the Brahmasūtra. The theistic character of reality also has its original lines in the Samhitās and later in the Upaniṣadas, specially the sectarian Upaniṣads. Thereafter the theistic nature and form of God was propounded by the Vaiṣṇavite Ācāryas, like Rāmānuja, Nimbārka, Vallabha and Madhva, commenting upon the Brahmasūtra, in their Bhāṣyas.

As indicated at the outset, to describe Viṣṇu as Trivikarma and Tripād in the Ṛgveda proves His universality as well as His all pervassiveness. The other attributes of Viṣṇu like His unequivellent powerfulness also prove him a supreme God, although in a Henotheistic manner. Decidendly the form of Paurāṇic Viṣṇu is different from the Ṛgvedic Viṣṇu, but not entirely and thus it may be said that the former has its roots in the Vedic mythological character of the diety. It may also be pointed out here that the Purāṇic mytholoy owes to the Vedic mythology in many ways. In fact, the Purāṇic thought does not have different line from the Vedas, instead of, it has made a full elaboration of the Vedic resurvoir of thought with its vividity and exaggeration, which is quite in a proper spirit :

"Itihāsa-purāṇābhyām Vedam Samupabṛṇhayet."

Regarding the Pantheism of the Purāṇas, Wilson seems to be quite fair when he says : "The Pantheism of the Purāṇas is one of their invariable characteristics, although the particular divinity, who is all things, from whom all things proceed, to whom all things return, be diversified according to their individual sectarial bias. They seem to have derived the notion from the Vedas; but in them, the one universal being is of a higher order than a personification of attributes and elements and however, imperfectly concerned or unworthily described, is God." As far as the position of Viṣṇu in the Viṣṇupurāṇa is concerned, it can be said, in a prematured way that it is based on the description of the Para and Apara Brahman of the Upaniṣads.

Befining Viṣṇu, the Viṣṇu Purāṇa says :

yasmādviśvamidaṃ sarvaṃ tasya śaktyā mahātmanaḥ.
tasmāt sa procyate viṣṇur viśa dhātoḥ praveśanāt.

In this verse, Viṣṇu is depicted as the creator who creates the universe with his unequivellent, Śakti.[1] It is called Viṣṇu, because it enters the universe, after creating it. It indicates further the allpervading character of Viṣṇu[2] and that He is undistinguished by place, time or property. Deshkālasvarūpatovyavacchedābhāvāt. Also the Padma Purāna mentions the same to say : "sa eva bhagavān viṣṇurprakṛtyāmāviveśaha. Basically, this is the principle of the Upaniṣads—

1. V.P. 3.1.45.
2. Viṣṇuśaktiranaupamyā V.P. 3.1.35.

and the later Vedānta.[1] According to the Vedāntic view, Bṛahman is the cause of creation, subsistence and dissolution. It may further be pointed out that Viṣṇu's entering into the universe, after creating it, proves Him as pure being, and thus without physique and it places Him parallel to the Vedāntic Brahman.

In Viṣṇu Purāṇa,[2] as initiated earlier, Viṣṇu has been described as determinate and indeterminate both as in Vedānta. Describing the nature and attributes of Brahman, the Viṣṇupurāṇa says that Viṣṇu is perfect, perpetual, universal, undecaying entire and uni-form. The Viṣṇu Purāna further says that a Yogin who attains this supreme truth (Brahman) does not take birth again and he gets deliverence from the distinction of virtue, vice, suffering and he becomes fully purified.[3] Thus Viṣṇu is Brahman, as quoted earlier and so none of the abovementioned attribute of Viṣṇu is against the nature of Brahman of Vedānta. To explain it further, it can be said that Vedānta mentions two states of Brahaman, the Para and Apara.[4] The Para is in—determinate and the Apara is determinate. Likewise, Viṣṇu

---

1. Janmādyasya yataḥ and the B S.S.B. 1.1.1.
2. Yadakṣaraṃ brahma ca Īśvaraḥ pumāṇ, V.P. 1 .1.2.
3. Yato nāvartate Punaḥ. Apunyapunyparame Kṣīṇaklesoti nirmalaḥ. V.P. 1,22,51, 52.

   Evam Prakāramamalam Nityam Vyāpakamakṣayam. Samastabhedarahitam Viṣnvākhyam Paramam Padam. Tad Brahma Paramam yogī.
4. Yatrāvidyākṛta nāmarūpādiviśeṣa-pratiṣedhād asthūlādi sabdair brahmopadiśyate, Tat-Pāram Tdeva Yatra nāmarupādi viśeṣeṇa kenacid viśiṣṭamu a diśyate ManomayaPrāṇa Śairo Bhārupaḥ, ityādi sabdais adaparaḥ (B.S.S.B. III. 14.2. IV. 3.14).

has two states, the Mūrtta and Amūrtta.[1] The Para Brahman is Akṣara and the Apara is Kṣara. The Gītā also describes the two states, the Akṣara and kṣara.[2] In Vedānta Brahman is substratum (Adhiṣthana) and nothing is apart from it and thus it is called the philosophy of Advaita. In the same way Vidyā and Avidyā, Sat and Asat and all else is neither Brahman and nothing is without as Radhakrishnan also explains.[3] The Viṣṇu Purāṇa has clearly admitted this Vedāntic way of interpretation.[4] The definition of Brahman given in Viṣṇupurāṇa,—*Dhruvamekākṣaram Brahma Omityevam vyavasthitam. Bṛhatvād Bṛṇhaṇattvācca Tad Brahmetyabhidhīyate*, which says that Brahman is eternal, monosyllabic and it is derived from the root Bṛha (to increase) is also quite similar to the derivation and definition of Bradman given by Śaṅkarācārya in his Brahmasutra—Bhāṣya.[5]

---

1. Dve rūpe brahmaṇastasya mūrttañcāmūr-ttamevaca. Kṣarākṣ-arasvarūpe te sarvabhūteṣū gīyate, V.P. 1.22.54.
2. Akṣaram Tat Param Brahma Kṣaram Sarvamidam Jagat, V.P. 1/22/55.
3. Rādhākrishnan Indian Philosophy, Vol. II.
4. Yā Vidyā yā tathāvidyā yat sad yaccāsadavyayam. Tat Sarvam Sarvabhūteśe Maitreya Madhusūdana. V.P. 1.22.77.

   Adhārah Sarvavidyānām Sayameva Harih Sthitah. DevaMānuṣapasvādisvarūpair bahubhih Sthitah.

   Tatah Sarveśvaronanto Bhūtomūr itiraṁūrttimān. V.P. 1.22.81.

   Ṛcho Yajūṇṣi Sāmāni Tathaivāthar Vaṇani-ca. Itihāsopavedāstu vedānteṣu Tathoktayah. V.P. 1.22.82.
5. Brahmaśabdasya hi Vyutpādyamānasya Nitya-śuddhatvādayorthāh Pratīyante, Bṛhaterdhātorar—thānugamāt. B.S.S.B. 1.1.1.

In Advaita-Vedānta, the world of duality is for the Ajñānins and in reality, Brahman and the world, are Advaita-swarūpa. The Viṣṇu Purāṇa also supports the view to say that all differences are due to the erroneous knowledge of people.[1] Thus the clear approach of Viṣṇu Purāṇa regarding Viṣṇu is that Vāsudeva, is the same with supreme spirit, which is Brahman.

Parama-Brahmaṇe tasmat nityameva namo namaḥ,
Yadrūpam Vāsudevasya Paramātmasvarūpiṇah. V.P. 3.3.27.

Like Brahman of the Vedānta, Viṣṇu is Jñānasvarūpa and supreme Bliss, Paramānanda.[2] The Jñāna is not the subject of exercise (Nirvyāpāram), is explained without the practice of abstract contemplation (Dhyānādiśūnyam), indescribable (Anākhyeyam), incapable of being enjoined Nirdesānarham) and internally diffused (Vyāptimātram)[3]. It is mental identification of individual with universal spirit Manasā Brahmākāratāmātraswarūpam" and it is self illumired (Ātmasaṃbodhaviṣayam). The Jñāna, which is sattāmātra is unmodified by the happenings of happiness. (Ānandādiviśeṣaśūnyam) and consequenty undefinable. It is tranquil (Praśantaṃ), void of passion (RāgādiŚūñyam), fearless, being nondual (Dvaitasphūrtterabhayam), and undisturbed by external objects (Nirviṣayaṃ). Moreover this supreme knowledge is never the theme of reasoning (Durvibhāvyaṃ) I can not be ascertained by logical deduction (Avitarkyaṃ) without any support and not depending upon perceptible objects (Nirviṣayatvadāśrayaśūnyam). Interest-

1. Sarva-bhūteṣvabhedos A bhidyate bhinna-buddhibhiḥ. V.P. 3.3.28.
2. Viṣṇorjñānamayasyoktaṃ tadjñānam Paramam Padam. V.P. 1.22.50.
3. Nirvyāpāramanākhyeyam vyāptimātramanupamam. Ātmasambodhaviṣayam Sattāmātramalakṣaṇam., Praśāntaṃ tamabhayaṃ Śuddhamavibhāvyamasaṇsṛ itam. V.P. 1.2?. 49, 50.

ingly all the above mentioned attributes of Jñāna also apply to the infinite knowledge advocated by the Vedāntin.

Although the aforesaid supreme concept of knowledge explained in the Viṣṇu Purāṇa is beyond all and supreme, the Purāṇa has also taken in view the other three types of spiritual knowledge. According to first, a yogin is essentially connected with and dependent upon, the means employed for emancipation.[1] The second type of knowledge is that which is acquired by the Yogin to escape from suffering to attain eternal felicity. (Paramānanda).[2] The third kind of knowledge is the ascertainment of the identity of the end and the means and the rejection of the notion of duality.[3] Here it is noteworthy that the supreme state of Viṣṇu, who is one with wisdom, is the knowledge of truth and that is the state of Mokṣa (Parama Pada). So to say in Vedānta, there too, the Brahmajñāna is Mokṣa.[4]

In this way, it may be observed that Viṣṇu cult as evinced in the Viṣṇu Puraṇa, has been elaborated on the line of Upaniṣadic Vedânta which is also very well similar to the Advaitic tenet enunciated by Saṅkarā-cārya. It may further be said that the Purāṇic treatment of Viṣṇu is much in line with the Vedic cult of Viṣṇu, as indicated earlier. It is needless to say that in the Viṣṇu Purāṇa, the mythological characterization, has given various shades to the pure image of Viṣṇu and this has presented Viṣṇu as Bhagawān and a Theistic God. Now it can be summarily said that the development of the Cult of Viṣṇu

1. Sādhanālambanam Jñānam Muktaye Yoginopi Tat, Sa bhedaḥ Prathamastasya Brahmabhūtasya, yoginaḥ V.P. 1.22.24.
2. Yuñjataḥ Kleśāmuktyartham sādhy-am yad Brahma yoginaḥ. Tadālambana. Vijñānam Dvitiyonśo Mahāmune. V.P. 1.22.46.
3. Ubhayastvaibhāgena Sādhya-Śādhanayorhi tat, Vijñā-namadvaitamayam Tadbhāgoo,nyo mayoditaḥ. V.P. 1.22.47.
4. Brahmaiva muktyavarthā, BrahmasūtraŚāṅkarabhāṣya.

can be divided in three stages : (1) the Ṛgvedic stage (2) the Brahamaṇic stage and (3) the epic and the Purāṇic stage. In its first stage, being among the group of sun gods. He is a subordinate god. Nevertheless in Ṛgveda, he has a significant pos tion. The third step of Viṣṇu, the Tripād is so high that no one can dare transgress and it is even beyond the flight of birds,[1] as the RV says. It further mentions, that the wise see the highest place of Viṣṇu.[2] (Paramampadam). According to the RV, Viṣṇu appears as the comrade and helper of Indra.[3] In Brāhmaṇic period, the position of Viṣṇu began to rise. In the Aitarya Brāhmana, Viṣṇu has been said the highest god and Agni the lowest.[4] The Śatapatha also describes Him as the highest god.[5] In the Maitrī Upaniṣad, interestingly, food has been called as the form of Viṣṇu which sustains the universe.[6] In the Kaṭha Upaniṣad, the progress of the human soul has been compared to a journey and the end of the path which he traverses, is the highest place (Parama-Padam) of Viṣṇu.[7] In the epic period, Viṣṇu grew to the state of supreme spirit. In the Mahābhārata, in chapters 65 and 66 of the Bhīṣma Paravan, the Supreme spirit is addressed as Nārāyaṇa and Viṣṇu is identified with Vāsudeva. As it goes to the Purāṇic age, it is the age of intermingling of the three religious thought as emerging (1) from Viṣṇu, the Vedic god at its source; (2) and Nārāyaṇa, the cosmic and philosophic god and (3) from Vāsudeva, the historical god. It is because of the same that various shades of the Viṣṇu cult are frequently found in Purāṇic literature specially in the Viṣṇu Purāṇa. Accordingly Viṣṇu's Brahmanic image has been presented presently.

---

1. R.V. 1.155.5.
2. R.V. 1.22-20.
3. See, Vaiṣnavism, Śaivism and minor-religious Systems, p. 33.
4. Aita, Brāhmaṇa, 1.1.
5. Śatapatha Brāhmaṇa, 14.1.1.
6. Maitri, Upa, V. 1.13.
7. Kaṭha Upa.

Madhvācarya-the Dvaitin

The prominent vaiṣnavite, Madhvācārya is a D-vaitavādin. His D vaitavāda is a reactionāry to the Viśiṣṭādvaitavāda concept of Rāmānujācārya and the Dvaitādvaitavāda of Nimbārkācārya Madhvācārya was also known by the names, Ānanda-tīrtha, Pūrṇaprajña-tirtha and vāsudeva. But his famous names are, Ānanda-tīrtha and Pūrṇaprajña. He was born in the year, 1197 and died in 1276, in the age of 79 ycars. Because he tried to wash away the Advaitavāda philosophy of Śaṅkarācārya, he was famous as an incarnation of Vāyu. His father was Madhyageha bhaṭṭa, who lived in the city, Rajatapīṭha, near Udipī. Rajatapīṭha is forty kilometrcs away from Śṛngerī in western direction. Udipī is a most prominent centre of Madhva philosophy. In Upipī, more than seventy thousand people are the followers of Madhva. Rajatapāṭha, the birth place of Madhva is known today as by the name of Kalyanpur. Acyutaprekṣa was the Guru of Madhva. It was at the time of Dīkṣā that Madhva was named as Purṇaprajña. First, he studied in depth the Advaita philosophy of Śaṅkara and thereafter refuted it. As Śaṅkara went from one place to another to propagate his philosophy of Advaita, like-wise Madhva for propagating his Dvaita and refuting Advaita, went to Viṣṇumaṅgala, to the southern side of Upipī - and then went to Anantpur, the present Trivendrum. There he had śāstric discussion & debates with the followers of Śaṅkarite Vedānta. Then he went to Dhanuṣkoṭi, and worshipped Viṣṇu. After this, the Ācārya turned to northern side and came to Haridwar and Badarikā-śrama. It is said that at Badarikāśrama, he met Vyāsa, who asked him to write a bhāṣya on the Brahmasūtra, in support of D-vaita philosophy. Then he returned to Udipī while he was returning to Udipī, at the bank of Godāvarī, he met Śobhana-bhaṭṭa, a staunch follower of Śaṅkara. It is also said that Madhva's guru, Ācyuta Prekṣa, who was an Advaitavādin in the beginning, became the follower of Dvaita philosophy. Ācārya Madhva wrote thirty seven works. Of them, Ṛgbhāṣya, Kramanirṇaya, Pūrṇa prajña-darśana, Aitareyo-paniṣad bhāṣya, Upanisadbhāṣya and the Mahābhārata tātparyanirṇaya, are very prominent.

Through his writings, Madhva propagated the phlio-sophy of Dvaita and refuted the Advaitic concept of Śaṅkara. It is thus that Madhava propounded the concept of Īś-vara, jīva, Jagat, Māyā and Mokṣa from D-vaita viewpoint. It would also be appropriate to say that the reactionary view to Śaṅara's philosophy, which was propounded by Rāmānujā-cārya was fully developed in Madhva's Dvaita philosophy. In other words, Śaṅkara's concept of Advaita was refuted by Rāmānujācārya and the philosophy of Viśiṣṭadvaita was established and then Nimbārka established the philosophy of D-vaitādvaita. But Madhva propounded the philosophy of Dvaita, contrary to his prior philosophical concepts.

The dualist Madhva propounded the independent identity of Īśvara and the world. Enunciating his D-vaita philosophy, Madhva established five types of difference: Difference between Īsvara and Jīva, Īsvara and the Jaḍa Jagat, the Jīva and Jagat, Jīva and the Jiva and Jaḍa and tha Jaḍa.[1] Finding a difference between Īsvara and Jīva, Madhva propounds that Isvara is omniscient and all-powerful, while Jīva is Alpajña and with limited power. Furthermore, the Jīva is enjoyer of the result of his good and bad actions.

---

1. See, Ghate, The Vedānta, p. 33.

In this regard, there seems a lacuna in the philosophy of Rāmānuja, according to which Jīva is the Aṁśa of Iśvara and therefore there arises a question that if Īśvarva also is the experiencer of the good and bad actions of the Jīva. This problem does not arise in Madhva philosophy, where Jīva & Īśvara are separate entities, as said above.

As far as the difference between Iśvara and the Jaḍa Jagat is concerned, both are different as Īśvara and the Jīva are different. While Īsvara is Cetana, the world is Acetana, Īśvara is creator, the world is created and Īśvara is controller, the world is controlled The main contribution of Madhva philosophy is that in it, the world is real, unlike Śāṅkara Vedānta which propounds that the world is false.

Madhva hac reasonably propounded the difference between Jīva and Jīva, because each individual has his own actions and has to enjoy the resul s of his actions. Thus Madhva is Anekajivavādin. As is apparent in the world, each jaḍa object is different from the other and therefore difference between the Jaḍa Padārthas, as enunciated by Madhva is appropriate. Thus the concept of D-vaita propounded by Madhva is more logical and convincing from the phenomenal point of view.

In Madhva philosophy, the treatment of Padārthas & Tattvas is different. Ācārya Madhva has admitted ten Padārthas and they are : Dravya, Guṇa, Karma, Sāmānya, Viśeṣa, Visiṣṭa, Aṁsī, Śakti, Sādṛsya and Abhāva. The Dravyas are twenty in number : Paramātma, Laksa, Jīva, Avyākṛta Ākāśa, Prakṛti, Guṇatraya, Mahatītva, Ahaṁkāra, Buddhi, Manas, Indriya, Mātrā, Bhūta, Brahmāṇda, Avidyā, Varṇa, Andhakāra, Vāsanā, Kāla and Prativimba. In addition to the Guṇas admitted by the Vaiśeṣikas, Madhva also admits some other Guṇas like Śama, Dama, Kṛpā, Titikṣā and Saundarya. There are three types of Karma in Madhva philosophy. These three types of Karma are, Vihita, Niṣiddha and Udāsīna. The Vihita Karmans are those which are recommended and justified by the Sāstras, while the Niṣiddha Karmans are those which are not justified by the Śāstras. The Udāsīna Karmans are those which are not to be compulsorily performed.

Madhva has admitted four types of Śaktis and they are : Acintya Śakti, Ādheya Śakti, Sahaj a Sāktl, and the Pada-Śakti. The Acintya Śakti of Paramātman, is extraordinary and with this Sakti, Paramātman performs the Alaukika Karmans. In an idol, the Sānnidhya of god is Ādheya—Śakti. In all the Padārths, the natural power is Sahaja Śakti. The Padaśakti exists in the Pada—Padārthas, in the form of Vācyavācaka bhāva.

In Madhva philosophy, Viṣṇu is Īsvara. As Madhva has explained, Viṣṇu is the cause of origin of Universe, subsistance and dissolution, controlling, Jñāna, Āvaraṇa, Bandhana and Mokṣa. According to Madhva, Īśvara is only Nimittakāraṇa and not Upādānakāraṇa. He has limitless virtues. Albiet, Īsvara is one in Madhva philosophy, he incarnates in many forms.[1] Lakṣmī is the Śakti of Paramātman.[2] It may be specially mentioned that although Lakṣmi appears separate from Viṣṇu, she is dependent on Him. Viṣṇu is above the material objects, the individual roots and Prakṛti. Madhva has mentioned the worship of Rāma & Śrīkṛsna, but he has never referred to the worship of Gopālakṛṣṇa, Vāsudeva & Rādhā. After Lakṣmī, the second important tattva, in Madhva philosophy, is Jīva. The Jiva is the subject of bondage and liberation. There are three types of Jīva, Mukti yogya, Nitya-samsā-rin and the Tamo yogya. The Muktiyogya Jīvas are of five types, Deva, Ṛṣi, Pitṛs, Cakravarttī and the Uttama Jīvas. The Nitya—Samsārin Jīvas are those, who get heaven and hell, according to their Karmans. These Jīvas are never

1. Avatārādayo viṣṇoḥ sarve pūrṇā prakīrtitāḥ.Pūrṇañca tat param pūrṇam pūrṅāt pūrṇaḥ Samudgataḥ.
2. Madhvasiddhāntarsāra, p. 26.

iiberated. The Daitya, Rākṣasa, Pisāca and the Jīvas of lower category, are Tamoyogya Jīvas.

In Madhva-thought, Avidyā is the cause of bondage and a hindrence in attaining liberation. As per the God's will, it veils the natural Jnana-Śakti of the Jīva and therefore, the Jīva is deprived of liberation. Madhva says that the Avidyā of each Jīva is individual.

Every philosophical system takes into account, the concept of Prakṛti or Māyā. In this regard, it may be said that Madhva's Māyá or Prakṛti is not false like the Māyā of Śaṅkarācárya, the Advaitin. Māyā, according to Madhva, acts as God desires and it is His power and the constituent cause of the world. As Madhva views upon in the beginning Kāla was originated from Prakṛti. Then God with his free will, created the Guṇatraya, the Sattva, the Rajas and the Tamas. After Mahat tattva, Ahaṁkāra is originated and after this, Manas, Indriyas and the five elements are originated. The five elements are five tanmātrās, in their perior state. In Madhva philosophy, the Ahamkāra is Vaikārika, Taijasa and Tämasa, because in it, Vikāra, Teja and Tamas exist.

The twenty four tattvas admitted by Madhva are Mahat, Ahaṁkāra, Buddhi, Manas, the ten senses, five tamātrās and five elements. There are two types of Buddhi, the S-varūpagata and the Jñānagat. Like-wise the Manas also is of two types the S-varūpa gata and the Indriya rūpa. In its Indriya rūpa, the Manas is eternal (Nityā) as well as mortal (Naśvara). In Madhva philosophy, Bhuddhi and Manas are also said as modes of mind. Manas is the cause of Saṁkalpa and Vikalpa and Buddhi is the deciding factor (Niscayātmikā). Ahaṁkāra is the base of egoistic feeling and the citta is the base memory. Contrary to other philosophical systems, Madhva admits twelve indriyas, the five karmendriyas, the five Jñānendriyas and Manas and the Sākṣī in Buddhi. In

Madhva thought, Sākṣin has a great significance. The Sākṣin is the enjoyer of pleasure and pain and the knower of time and space (Deśa and Kāla). Madhva admits Sāksi-Jñāna as the cause of Anubhūtisvarūpa-jñāna and in his view, it is also the cause of the knowledge of time and space, unavoidably. In addition to this, in Madhva philosophy, the Sākṣin witnesses the multifarious knowledge of the Indriyas, on one side and on the other, it is Sākṣin of its I—hood (Ahantā). It is also to be specially mentioned that in Madhva philosophy, the self realization is not the subject of Manas or mental experience, instead of, it is the subject of the experience of Sākṣin.

If Ātmānubhūti is admitted as the subject of Manas, which is saṅkalpa-vikalpātmaka, then Ātmānubhūti also would be admitted like-wise, which is not desirable.

Mokṣa is the supreme attainment of a man and it has been differently taken into account in the systems of Indian philosophy. While the Advaitins propounded that the realization of indeterminate Brahman, is Mokṣa, the Vaiṣṇavas mainly admit Mukti, as sāyujya, sāmīpya, sālokya Mukti. and sārūpya. Of them, Madhva is the supporter of sāmīpya-In Madhva philosophy, Jīva has the Sākṣātkāra of Viṣṇu and attains the supreme bliss. For the realization of Viṣṇu, there are mentioned eighteen means to attain it and they are : (i) Vairāgya, (ii) Sewā (iii) Sāstric knowledge, (iv) Śaraṇāgat', (v) to be at the feet of Guru, (vi) to attain knowledge from the Guru, (vii) to follow the teachings of Guru, (viii) to respect the teachers, devotees and scholars, (ix) Paramätma bhakti, (x) To respect youngers, to have sincere Śraddhā for elders, (xi) to perform sacrifice, without having a desire, (xii) to renunciate the prohibited karmans, (xiii) to do Samarpaṇa of all the karmans to God (xiv) to understand the Svarūpa-Jñāna of Viṣṇu as the supreme, (xv) to realize the difference of Īśvara and the world, Īśvara and the Jīva, Jīva and the world, Jīva and Jīva and the Jaḍa and Jaḍa, (xvi) to realize a difference between Prakṛti and Puruṣa, Jīva and Bhagawān, the Jīva and the Jaḍa Padārthas, (xvii) To disagree with false and baseless doctrines and (xvii) the Upāsanā. In Madhva philosophy, the Upāsanā is of two types, the study of the Śāstras and the Dhyāna or Nididhyāsana. In this way, the Madhva philosophy, the eighteen Sādhanas help a man for the realization of Śrī Bhagawān Viṣṇu.

As has been mentioned above the contribution of Madhva to Indian philosophy, is remarkable. The Viṣṇu cult which has its origin in the Ṛgveda and its further elaboration in the Purāṇas particularly the Viṣṇu Purāṇas, is the basic essential of the Vaiṣṇavite philosophy. The Vaṣṇavite Ācāryas, prominently, Rāmānuja, Madhva, Nimbārka and Vallabha, have propounded their systems, Visiṣṭādvaita Vāda, Dvaitavāda, Dvaitādvaitavāda and Śuddhādvaitavāda, respectively. To comment, on the Brahmasūtra of Bādarāyaṇa Vyāsa, opposing the Advaita—vedānta of Saṅkarācārya, among the above mentioned four Vaiṣṇavite Ācāryas, Madhva, being a Dvaitin is much more opposite to the philosophy of Śaṅkara, the Advaitin.

Many a post-Madhva Ācārya had a great impact of Madhva's view on them. Of them, Padmanābha tīrtha, Naraharitīrtha, Madhvatīrtha, Akṣobhaya tīrtha, Jayatīrtha, Vidyādhirāja'tīrtha, Kavīndratīrtha, Vāgisatīrtha, Rāmachandratīrtha, Vidyānidhitīrtha, Raghunātha tīrtha, Raghuvaryatīrtha, Raghūttamatīrtha, Vedavyāsatīrtha, Vidyādhīśatīrtha and Satya-Vrata tīrtha, may be specifically mentioned.

There are two aspects of Bhakti as propounded by Madhva: (1) It developes sense of politeness, negoistic feeling, broadness and servicible nature on one hand and strengthens the attitude of Bhakta towards the Māhātmyā, Audātya, and Aiśvarya of Śrī-bhagawān. This twin-streamed flow of Bhakti as maintained by Madhva, is a noteworthy view of the Bhakti school.

Vedānta and other orthodox philosophical systems

It is well-known that on the basis of the philosophical thought of the Upaniṣads, the six systems, Nyāya, Vaiśeṣika, Saṁkhya, Yoga and Vedānta have originated. This is the revealing power of the Ṛṣis like Gotama that they formalized their philosophical systems like Nyāya on the founding of Informal revelations, prevalant in the Upaniṣads. But it may be stressed upon that the sole aim of all the six systems is to attain the real khowledge, the base of supreme peace or bliss, or to get heaven or Mokṣa. All the six systems admit Avidyā or ignorance as a hindrance in the way of achieving the final good. To illustrate, it may be said that like Vedānta, Nyāya also admits false knowledge as the cause of bondage.[1] The Nyāya-sūtra also says that the real knowledge (Tattvajñāna) is the cause of Niḥśreyasa.[2] The Vedānta also enunciates that Mukti is never possible, without Jñāna. As far as the cause of world is concerned, the Naiyāyika says that it is Aṇu, while the Vedānta in propounds that the Māyā is the constituent cause of the world. This view has been expressed by Vijñāna bhikṣu in his yoga vārttika, quoting the Vṛhadvāśiṣṭha :

Nāmarūpa-vinir muktam yasmin santiṣṭhate Jagat,
Tamāhuḥ prakṛtim Kecin Māyāmanye paretvaṇum.

---

1. Duḥkha-Janma-pravṛttidoṣa-mithyā-jñānānām uttarot tarāpāye tadanantarāpāyādapavargaḥ.

N.S. 1.1.1.

2. ......Tattvajñānān niḥsreṣādhigamaḥ. N.S. 1.1.2.

Regarding Mukti, it may be said that the state of Mukti in Nyāya and Vedānta is quite similar to some extent. As udyotakara, the Naiyāyika observes there are two types of Mukti, the Apara niḥśreyesa and the Paraniḥśreyasa. Explaining Aparaniḥśryesa, he says that one attains it after the Tattvajñāna[1], the real knowledge. Clearly, this is the state of Jīvan-mukti of the Vedānta. Śaṅkara says that even the Jīvanmukta has to live in this world for experiencing the result of his Karman.[2] Explaining Paraniḥśreyasa, Vācapati in his Tātparya tikā says that it can only be attained after the enjoyment of Prārabdha-Karmans.[3] So also, Śaṅkara mentions that even the liberated has to live in his present body till the enjoyment of his Prārabdha Karmans. The Upaniṣadas also mention the idea of Jīvanmukti and Videhamukti, as earlier also said. Thus it may be said that the Naiyāyika has borrowed the idea of Jīvanmukti and Videhamukti from the Upaniṣadic Vedānta. However the state of Mukti in Nyāya and Vedānta is to be further taken in view. The Nyāya holds that completely to get rid of all pains, is Apavarga. Thus the Naiyāyika does not admit the blissful state of Mukti, as the Vedāntin does. (Rasovai saḥ). But it may be said that the Duḥkhābhāva-state of Mukti admitted by the Naiyāyika obviously proves

---

1. Yattāvadaparam nīḥsresan tattvajñānānantaramevabhavati.

   Nyāya vārttika 1.1.1.

2. B.S.S.B. 4.1.15.
3. Paraniḥśresamatonyat bhavatiyadupabhogādupātta-Karmāsayapracayo na kṣīyate.

   Tātparya-tīkā, P. 81

4. See, ehā. Upa. 4/14/3 & Bṛha. upa. 4.4.8.
5. Ten duḥkhena Janmanā atyantam vimukti rapa-vargaḥ. Vātsyāyana's bhāṣya on the N.S. Tadatyanta vimokṣopavargaḥ.

the state of bliss, for to get rid of pains, in directly supports the state of bliss. In this regard, thus, Das Gupta's view[1], that the state of liberation can not be admitted as the state of bliss, is not proper. Therefore, it is evident that there is direct and indirect impact of Upaniṣadic Vedānta on

the concept of Mokṣa as propounded by the Naiyāyika.

So also, the Vaiśeṣika has the Vedāntic impact. The Avidyā or Māyā which is major concept of Advaita Vedānta, also has been referred and explained by Kaṇāda in his Sūtras.[2] Further to illustrate, Praśastapāda, the commentator of the Vaiśeṣika sūtra, taking into account the Vidyā and Avidyā first finds four categories of Vidyā, Pratyakṣa, Laingika Smṛti and Arṣa.[3] But he also includes Avidyā in Vidyā and says that the Vidyä also is of two types, the Vidyā and Avidyā and there are four categories of Avidyā, Samasaya, Viparyaya, Anadhyavasāya and the S-vapna.[4] Here it may be interestingly noted that the Viparyaya of Vaiśeṣika is like the Adhyāsa of the Vedāntin. As Praśastapāda says that the knowledge of unreal in something real is Viparyaya,[5] likewise, the Vedāntin, defining Adhyāsa says that the superimposition of unreal on real is

1. S.N. Das Gupta, A History of Indian philosophy, Vol. I.P. 366.
2. See, Vaiśeṣika sūtra, 7.1.21 & 9.2. 10.
3. Vidyāpi caturvidhā Pratyakṣalaiṅgika smṛtyārṣalakṣaṇā Praśastapāda-bhāṣya, Buddhinirūpaṇa, P. 552. (Chowkhamba).
4. Tasyā satyapyaneka, Vidhatve samāsato dve vidy-vidya cāvidyā ceti. Tatrāvidhā caturvidhā samśaya-viparyay-ānadhyavasya svapnalakṣaṇā, Praśastapada-bhāṣya, Buddhi nirūpaṇa, P. 520.
5. Atasmin stadete pratyayo viparyayaḥ, Praśastapāda-bhāsya, P. 538.

Adhyāsa or Āropa. Thus, the notion of Avidyā and Māyā is quite similar in Vaiśeṣika and Vedānta.[1]

Although the Sāṁkhya view is dualistic and realistic, it is also quite similar to Vedānta and Sāṁkhya, both are Upaniṣadic, basically. The concept of Puruṣa and Prakṛti of the Sāṁkhya, has its clear roots in the Upaniṣads. The Kaṭha mentions Puruṣa superior to Avyakta.[2] The Śvetāśvatara clearly mentions of Prakṛti.[3] These concepts find a prominent place in Vedānta. The Ātman of Vedānta is very near to Puruṣa of Sāṁkhya. As is Sāṁkhya, the Puruṣa is one[4] as well as many, so in Vedānta,[5] Ātman is enunciated as the supreme reality and the Jīvātman as the Kariā & Bhoktā. The Sāṁkhya also describes Puruṣa as Bhokṭṛ.[6] As far as the state of liberation in the two schools is concerned, it is also similar to a certain extent. In Saṁkhya, in the state of liberation, the liberated is not attached to Prakṛti[7] & likewise in Vedānta the liberated fully gets rid of Māyā the cause of duality and bondage. As in Vedānta, in the state of Mukti, it remains only the knowledge of Ātman or Brahman, in the same way, Mukti, according to Sāṅkhya

---

1. Adhyāso nāma-atasminstadbuddhiḥ. B.S. S.B. 1.11.
   Vastunyavastvāropo' adhyāropaḥ, Vedāntasāra, P. 13.
   (Chowkhamba.
2. Avyaktāt puruṣaḥ paraḥ.
   Kaṭha, 3.11.
3. Māyām tu prakṛtim vidyāt.
   Śveta. Upa. 1.4.3.
4. Vyaktāvyaktajña-vijñānāt. S.K.2.
5. Puruṣavah utvam siddham.
   S.K. 18.
6. Puruṣo'stibhokṭṛ-bhāvāt.
   S.K. 17.
7. Prakṛtim paśyati puruṣaḥ. prekṣakavadavasthitaḥ susthaḥ.
   S.K. 65.

is the state of Kevalajñāna.[1] The concept of Jīvanmukti and Videhamukti also is similar in Vedantā and Sāṁkhya. Regarding Jīvanmukti, the Sāṁkhya view is that as even after stopping the potter's wheel, it continues to take rounds[2], so even after attaining liberation, the liber ated performs the Prārabdha Karmans. When the performance of the Prārabdhakarmans is over, the liberated becomes Videhamukta. But there are also some dissimilarities, between two. For example, the illusory character of Māyā of the Vedāntin, is not admissibe to and the follower of Sāṁkhya. Similarly, the theory of causation of the two also different. The Vedāntin is Vivartavādin, while the Sāṁkhya supports the view of Satkāryavāda. Secondly, the creator, Īśvara, in Vedānta is Abhinnanimittopādānakāraṇa which is not acceptable to Sāṁkhya. In Saṁkhya, the creation is due to the joining of Prakṛti & Puruṣa. However it may be said that neither Īś-vara of the Vedānta and nor the Puruṣa of Sāṃkhya is competent to create without Māyā and Prakṛti, respectively.

The Yoga may be said as the practical side of the Vedānta. It is also very near to Sāṁkhya.[3] In Vedānta, controlling of senses, is unavoidably necessary, because without it, tranquility of mind[4] is not possible, which is very much desired for attaining liberation. The Yoga also lays more stress on the controlling of mode of mind ('yogaś-cittavṛtti-

---

1. Kevalamutpadyate jñānam.

S.K, 64.

2. Cakrabhramivad dhṛtaśarīrah.

S.K. 67.

3. Sāṁkhyayogau pṛthagbalāḥ pravadanti na paṇḍitāḥ.

B.G.

4. Praś-āntacittāya jitendriyā-ya ca prahiṇadosāya yathoktakāriṇe. Guṇānvi tay-ānugatāya sarvadā pradeyametatsatatam mumukṣave.

U.S., Pārthiva prakaraṇa, 72.

nirodhaḥ, Y.S. 1.1.). A later Vedāntin, Sadānanda also mentions, Śama, Dama, Uparama, Titikṣā, Samādhāna and Śraddhā as the prerequisites for the Adhikārin of the Vedānta-Vidyā.

As has been evident, Avidyā is a significant doctrine of Advaita Vedānta and it also occupies an important place in Yoga philosophy. In Vedānta, Adhyāsa and Avidyā are the same.[1] As earlier also has been mentioned, Śaṅkara defines Adhyāsa, to say—"Adhyāsonāma tasminstad buddhiḥ." Likewise, in Yoga also, the definition of Avidyā is "Atasminstatpratibhāsah".[2] In Saṅkara Vedānta, the Vikṣepa Śakti of Avidyā is the cause of all mental confusions and afflictions.[3] Similarly, the Yoga also admits Avidyā as the origin of ihood & egoism.[4] The Yoga also admits Avidyā as the cause of all afflictions.[5] According to Vidyāraṇya, Māya is the creating power as well as the power of keeping people in delusion.[6] In the same manner, the Bhojavṛtti also mentions Avidyā as the delusion.[7] This way, the Avidyā of Vedānta and the Yoga is quite similar. The Īśvara tattva is most prominent in both the systems, the Yoga and Vedānta. In both the systems, Īśvara is the creator of the universe. But it may be pointed out that in Vedānta, it is Māyā, due to, which Īśvara is the creator[8], while in Yoga,

1. Adhyāsam paṇḍitā avidyeti manyante.
B.S. B.1.1.1.
2. B.S.S. B.1.1.1.
3. Ragādayo'syā prabhavanti nityam duhkhādayo ye manaso Vikārāḥ Vivekacūḍāmaṇi, P. 113.
4. Avidyā Kṣetram prasavabhū-miruttareṣāmasmitādīnām.
Yogabhāṣya, 2.4.
5. Bhojavṛtti, 2.4.
6. Pañcadaśī, 4.12.
7. Avidyā Mohaḥ. Bhojavṛtti, 2.4.
8. Nahi tayā vinā Parameś-varasyasrṣṭṛtvam sidhyati.
B.S. S.B. 1.4.3.

Īs-vara creates the universe, by His mere will. Īśvara as admitted in Yoga, is Puruṣa—Viśeṣa. Now let us consider Mukti, the supreme aim of man, according to Indian philosophy, with regard to Yoga and Vedānta. The Yoga and Vedānta, both are the believers of Jīvamnmukti & Videhamukti. But the concept of Jīvanmukti is not as clear in Yoga, as in Vedānta, as Maxmuller also says.[1]

By the said analysis, it is clear that the yoga and Vedānta are complementary to each other and a way they are two aspects of the same philosophical system.

So far as the Purva mīmāmsa is concerned, it is the prior aspect of to Vedānta & thus its completion can be found in Vedānta[2]. The principle of Karma and Dharma also is not entirely contrary to Vedānta, as through the Dharma, one gets his heart purified which is essential for the realization of self. Allthough the Mīmāṃsā & Vedānta, are quite contradictory, still there are many similar points between the two. To illustrate, Laugākṣi Bhāskara says that any work, performed, dedicating it to God, becomes the cause of

---

1. Secondly, the Puruṣa though freed from illusion, is not thereby annihilated. He is himself, apart from nature and it is possible, though it is not distinctly stated that the Puruṣa in his aloneness may continue his life, like the Jīvanmukta of the Vedānta, maintaining his freedom among a crowd of slaves, without any fear or hope of another life unchanged himself in this everchanging Saṃsāra. Maxmuller, Indian Philosophy, Vol. III, P. 143.
2. For the line of thought commenced by the Mīmāṃsā is completed by Vedānta, which constitutes the last word, on the problem of the soul, with reference to both, knowledge and action.

   N.V. Thadāni, Mīmāṃsā, Introduction, P. cxi.

Niḥśreyasa.[1] The Vedānta also holds the same view.[2] Here, it will not be inappropriate to mention that the concept of Brahman was developed on the basis of Pantheism of the Vedas.

Regarding Mokṣa, it may be said that the end of relation with world phenomenons, is Mokṣa, according to Mīmāṃsā[3]. The cause of Prapañca is Avidyā, & when Avidyā is removed after the Brahmajnāna, the relation with Prapañca also is ceased.[4] The Vedāntā also supports the view that after Brahmajñāna, Avidyā, the cause of all prapañca comes to cessation.[5]

As it has been seen obove, by the similarities, between Vedāntic concepts and the concepts of other five orthodox systems, it is evident that the Vedānta has left an impact on the aforesaid five systems of Indian philosophy and it is because all the systems have their origin in the Upaniṣads & Vedānta is the main Upaniṣaidic philosophy.

---

1. Īśvarārpaṇabuddhyā Kṛyamāṇan tu niḥsreyasahetuḥ Arthasaṁgraha, P. 169.
2. S.B. Gītā, 9.28.
3. Prapañca-sambandha-Vilayo-Mokṣaḥ Ṣāstra dīpikā, P. 357.
4. Avidyānirmito hi prapañchaḥ svapnaprapañcavat prabodhanenaiva brahmavidyayā avidyā, vilināyam svameva viliyat Śāstra dipikā, P. 359.
5. Vidyayā tasyāḥ bījaśakterdābāt B.S.S B. 1.4. 3.

The Philosophy of Grammer

Like other systems of Indian philosophy, the final aim of the philosophy of Grammer also is to know the reality, the base of the universe or the Śabda—Brahman. The base of the philosophy of Grammer is Vāk-tattva, which is prevalent in the earliest text, the Ṛgveda.[1] Therein, the Vāk has been mentioned as Kāmadhenu. At another place, in the Ṛgveda, many forms of the Vāk tattva have been indicated.[2] The Ṛgveda also says that Brahman is the base of the Vāk-tattva and that is the ultimate truth.[3] According to the Atharvaveda, the Vāk has been mentioned as Prajāpati and the creator of Daivī and Āsuri crearion.[4] The Aaitareya Brāhmaṇa also mentions Vāk as the cause of Artha-tattva.[5] This can be said as the foundation of the philosophy of word and meaning. The Upaniṣads also mention the Vāk as Para-Brahman[6]. In the seventh chapter of the chāndogyopaniṣad, Sanat Kumāra describes Vāk as the base of all thinking Accordingly, neither Dharma, nor Adharma, neither truth nor untruth and neither good nor bad could be possible. Sanat Kumāra

---

1. Ṛgveda, 8-100-11.
2. Vacā virūpanityayā.
3. See Ṛgveda, 1.164.34, 35.
4. Atharvaveda, 19.9.3.
5. Vāk yoniḥ, Aitareya-Brāhmaṇa, 2.38.
6. Bṛhadāraṇyaka Upaniṣad, 4.1.

further tells to Nārada, that whosoever worships Vāk as Brahman, he has a control over it. In Upaniṣadic Vedānta, there is a description of the Pañcakosas and likewise the grammarians also have taken in view the significance of the Pañcakosas, the Annamaya, the Prāṇamaya, the Manomaya, the Vijñānamaya and the Ānandamaya. For example, Bhaṭṭojīdīkṣita in his Vaiyākaraṇa—bhūṣana, Kaunḍa bhaṭṭa in his Viyākaraṇa – bhūṣaṇa sāra, Sri Kṛṣṇabhaṭṭa in his Sphotacandrikā and many other grammarians have taken into account the five sheaths of Indian philosophy. The grammarians compare the Varṇasphoṭa with Annamaya Kośa, the Padasphoṭa with Prāṇamaya Kosa and the Vākyasphoṭa with Manomayakośa. Albiet, primarily they are Akhanḍavākyasphoṭavādins. They also admit Jātivākya sphoṭa. In this way, the grammarians have propounded the Brahman as Nitya, Nirañjana, Ajara, Amara and Akṣara. As in Vedānta philosophy, the five sheaths are the systematic steps for attaining Brahman, the same way, in the philosophy of grammer, the Varṇajñāṇa, Padajñāna, Vākyajñāna and Akhanḍajñāna and Brahmajñāna, are attained systematically.

By the above point of viewing, it is evident that the philosophy of grammer has its clear origin in the Vedic literature. As far as sphoṭa, the soul of Grammetical philosophy is concerned, Pāṇini made its first use in the Aṣṭādhyāyī (6.1.123) to refer sphoṭāyana is understood as the propounder of Sphoṭa.

There are a number of Ācāryas and commentators, who have contributed to the field of philosophy of grammer. The commentator of the Vākyapadīya, Helarāja, has mentioned Ācārya Rāvaṇa as the first Ācārya of the philosophy of grammer. It may be mentioned, that Bhartṛhari wrote the Vākyapadīya, on the basis of the teachings, he received from his teacher, Vasurāta,

Among the Ācāryas of the philosophy of grammer, the names of Sphotayana, Audumbarāyaṇa, Vyāḍi, Patañjali, Bhartṛhari, Vṛṣabhadeva, Dharmapal, Punyarāja, Helārāja, Phullarāja, Gangādāsa, Maṇḍana Miśra, Parameśvara, Bharatamiśra, Harivallabha, Hari Bhaṭṭa, Mannu Deva, Bhairava miśra, Rudra-nātha, Brahmadeva and Jagdisha Tar kālaṅkara are highly worthmentioning. Among the Ācāryas, Pāṇini, Vyāḍi and Patañjali have contributed enormously to the field of grammer. Pāṇini is the believer of śabdanityatva and the supporter of the Sphoṭa theory, After Pāṇini, Vyāḍi is the main Ācārya who was also known by the name of Dākśayaṇa. Ācārya Vyāḍi's main work is Saṁgraha, which was appreciated by Patañjali, to call it ' Śobhana Kṛti". In the Samgraha, the Nityatva and Anityatva of Sabda has been taken into account. the Samgraha contained one lac verses.

Puruṣottamadeva mentions three names of Vyāḍi and they are ; Vidhyastha, Nandinī, sūta and Medhāvi. Vyāḍi, the author of Samgraha has been referred to in many works like Ṛgprati rakhya. Thus undoubtedly, Saṁgraha is an authentic work of Vyādi. It may be further said that jitendra buddhi the writer of Nayā a has referred five vacanas from the Saṁgraha of Vyāḍi and also Kaiyata, in his Mahābhāṣya—pradipa has referred to Saṁgraha. Hardatta in his Padamanjari quotes the verses of Saṁgraha right times. It is further interesting to no e that according to VālmīkiRāmāyaṇa, Bhakta Hanumān studied the Saṁgraha.

"Sasūtravṛtyarthapadam mahārthamasamgrahamsidhyati vai kapindraḥ".

Patañjali

Patañjali, through his contribution of the Mahābhāṣya, has presented his grammetical philosophy in a very easy and lucid way. Patanjali is known by many names like Goṇadiya,

Goṇikaputra, Ahipati, Phanibhṛta, Śeṣarāja, Śeṣāhi, Cūrṇi-kāra and Padakāra.

Albiet, in the Mahābhāṣya, the principles of Pāṇinian grammer are mainly explained, there are also taken into account the views of grammerians, who were prior to Patañjali.

Patañjali is the propounder of Śabdanityatva. He says that in a Nitya-śabda, the varṇa should be Kutartha, Nirupa, Niranjana and Acala and thus there is no scope for any vikāra in the varṇa. It may be said that Patanjali is clearly the Sphotavādin. Defining Sphota, Patañjali says that which is heard by Srotra, known through intellect, expressed through pronouncing and has its place in Ākāsa, is Śabda—sphota. Taking in to account, the Sphoṭa and Dhram, Patañjali says, that the sphoṭa is its guṇa and both exist in Śabda. Then is Vyangya-vyanjaka bhāva in Dhvani and sphota and the former is vyanjaka and the later is Vyangya, according to Patañjali.

Bhartṛhari

Bhartṛhari (700 A.D.) is most prominent, among the Ācaryās of philosophy of grammer. He is also known as the brother of Vikramāditya and he is also known as a Yogin. There is a cave in Ujjaiyinī, which is famous as "Bhartṛharig hā. This also proves Bhartṛhari as a Yogin. There are found six prominent works by Bhartṛhari and they are : Mahābhā-ṣyadīpikā, Vākyapadīya, the commentary or the Vākyapa-diya, Bhaṭṭikāvya, Bhāgavṛtti and the Subha ita tri ati. The Mimāṃsa bhāṣya, Vedāntasūtra Vṛtti and Śabdadhātu samīkṣā are also said as the works by Bhartṛhari.

Bhartṛhari's philosophical level is wellknown as Śabdādvaitavāda. According to Śabdādvaitavāda, Śabda, Brahman is Anādi and Ananta and the world is the manifestation (vivarta) of Sabda Brahman.[1] In Advaita Vedānta also, the world is described as the Vivarta of Brahman. Therefore, this way, the impact of Vedānta on Bhartṛhari's philosophy is cvident. As sabda Brahmavādin propounds, sabda brahma controles the origin and expression of the whole world through its free Kāla-Sakti. Bhartrhari maintains that it is through Vyākaraṇa that Sabda brahman is known and thereafter Mokṣa is attained. In Bharthari's philosophy of word and meaning, the word and meaning and their relation is Nitya. Bhartṛhari admits five Pramānas : Pratyakṣa, Anumāna, Śabda, Abhyāsa and Adṛṣṭa.

The essence of Bhartṛhari's philosophy is Sphoṭa, which is Nimitta as well as Arthabodhaka. Sphoṭa is the Nimitta Vaikharī and the vaikharī is pronounced for the Arthabodha. Thus the Sphoṭa is Artha bodhaka, as a matter of fact.

The process of creation, as explained in the philosophy of grammer, is that in the beginning, the Paśyanti Vāk as Brahman, contemplates to create the world of name and form through its Māyāśakti and afterwards through its Kāla-Śakti creates the five elements, the Ākāśādi.

Regarding creation, Nāgeśa has a different opinion. He says that in Pralaya, the Karmans which are subject to experience, are destructed and then the world is dissolved into Īśvara. Here, by dissolution, Nāgeśa understands the state of Suṣupti. Nāgeśa further maintains that first of all, in Īśvara, Māyā, which is the seed power of creation, is originated and afterwards, the Śakti tattva, which is unmanifest triguṇa bindu, is created. The bindu has three parts, i.e. cidaṃśa, cidacidaṃśa and the Nādacidaṃśa. The Nāda is Parā Vāk. Bhartṛhari, the author of Vākyapadīya has propounded Nāda as Śabda Brahman.

---

1. Anādinidhanam Brahma śabdatattvam yadakṣaram.
Vivarte,rthabhāvena prakṛyā jagato yataḥ.
Vākyapadīya, 1.1.

It is the essence of Śabda brahman philosophy that Vāk is Brahman and it is the basic source of creation. The Vāk, originally is of three types, Paśyantī, Madhyamā and Vaikharī. Each one of the three is again of three types, the Sthūla, the Sūkṣma and the Parā. In this manner, the Vāk is of nine types. The main Vāk is said like the sun and its twelve varieties are mentioned as the raises of the sun. As the sun brings to light the worldly objects, the same way, the vāk-Brahman, illumines the whole universe.

In the philosophy of Grammer, the concept of Pratibhā has been specifically mentioned. According to Nāgeśa, Pratibhā has been mentioned as Vākyārtha. In each individual, the pratibhā exists differently. The Pratibhā also exists in animals and birds. It is natural as well as created. As the Śabdabrahmavādin propounds, Śabda is the cause of Pratibhā. It is a different matter whether the cause of Pratibhā, is the Śabda, experienced in this life or the last life.

Furthermore, in the philosophy of Śabda Brahmavāda, there are experienced two standards of Jñāna, the Samyak Jñāna and the Samyak prayoga. Grammer is the Śāstra of Samyak-jñāna and Sāhitya is the Śāstra of Samyak-prayoga. It may be said that both are necessary for the fruitfulness of the Śabda. It is therefore that Patañjali says in the Mahābhāṣya :

"Ekaḥ śabdaḥ samyak jñātaḥ, suṣṭhu prayuktaḥ Svarge Loke ca Kāmadhug bhavati".

If we have a comparative view regarding the philosophy of grammer, it may be compared with the concept of Siddhānta-Śaiva and the Vedāntic concept of Śaṅkara, the

Brahmavādin. In Sid lhāta Śaiva philosophy, there are three main tattvas. The Jñānas warūpiṇī śakti is Śiva, the Parigraha Śakti (Bindu) of Śiva which is also called the Kṛyā Śakti and the Ātman. The Saivaite Ācaryas admits two types of Bindu, the pure Mahāmāya and the impure Māyā. Vāk is the Pariṇāma of both the Bindus. According to Siddhānta-Śaiva, the Atikrama of Vāk is Mokṣa. Abhinava-Gupta is also Śaiva. In his opinion, Prakāśa and Vimarśa, the two tattvas are admitted. The Prakāśa tattva is Śiva and the Vimarśa is S-vatantra Śakti and this Śakti is Umā. The Prakāśa and Vimarśa, the two are one, as a matter of fact. As Abhinava Gupta says, the Vimarśa is Parāvāk and the Prakāśa is Artha.

As far as the Vedāntic concept of Śaṅkara is concerned, Brahman is self-illumined, but it is not like Vimarśa of the Śaiva. It is due to Māyā that Brahman appears in many worldly forms. The Avidyā of the Vedāntin is Anirvacanīyā. Also according to the śabda-Brahmavāda concept, the Śabda Brahman appears in many forms.

It may be further emphasized that according to Śabda-Brahmavādin, Paśyanti Vāk is Śabda Brahman and the tādātmya of Jīva in Śabda Brahman, is Mokṣa. It may also be mentioned here that even in the state of Mokṣa, the Jīva exists as Śabdātman. But so far as the Siddhānta-Śaiva mata is concerned, in the state of Mokṣa, it remains only the Śuddhāvāk. In this state, there is appearance of cit and the vāk is known as cidrūpiṇī. It may be further said that in Siddhānta-Śaiva, the tādātmya of Jīva with Vāk is not admitted.

In nutschell, Śabda is most significant tattva in the philosophy of Grammer. In this regard, Bhartṛhari says that the fire of the wooden piece becomes the cause of outer fire, like-wise Śabda becomes the cause of different Śrutis ;

Araṇistham yathā jyotiḥ prakāśāntara Kāraṇam.
Tadvacchabdo'pi buddhisthaḥ śrutīnām kāraṇam mahat.

Therefore, it may be said that according to the philosophy of grammer, Śabda-Saṃskāra is the means of Brahma-siddhi and thus only he who knows the Saḍbhāva-vikāra, the Śabda-brahma-pravṛtti, and the Pratibhā tattva, can attain the Brahma tattva and nobody else.

Vivekānanda : An Advocate of Hinduism

According to Vivekánanda, Hinduism is another name of Vedānta, the concept of one soul (Ātman), in all beings. He says : "*The one central idea of Vedanta is oneness. There are no two in any thing, no two lives, nor even two different kinds of life for the two worlds......The Vedānta entirely denies such ideas as that animals are separate from man, and that they were made and created by God to be used for our food*". (*The complete works of Swami Vivekananda, Vol. II* (p. 295). Hinduism is as old as the Vedas and the Upaniṣads. In the Ṛgveda, the oldest text, the one soul idea is found in the Mantra" एकं सद् विप्रा बहुधा वदन्ति (The one reality is expressed in many ways, by the Vipras.) During his conversation with a disciple, in the year, 1898, at the Belur Math, Vivekananda said :

"Brahman is one, but is at the same time appearing to us as many, on the relative plane".[1]

The one reality concept of the Vedas can be said as the base of the Upaniṣadic Ātman and far later of the Śaṅkarite Advaita, the pioneer of Hinduism and Advaita Śaṅkarācārya, the Advaitin, propounded, with an exposition, the tenet of Ātman or Brahman in every body. This makes a developed base for Hinduism. One should not hesitate to admit that

1. The complete works of Swāmī Vivekānanda, vol. VII, p. 95.

the Vedānta or Hinduism propagated by Śaṅkarāchārya could not be much practised, because of its scholastic apprcach. Thus it was Vivekānanda, who laid more stress on practical Vedānta, which he considered the advocate of human service and world brotherhood. He says :

"*If it is absolutely impracticable, no theory is of any value whatever, except as intellectual gymnastics.*"[1]

Vivekānanda very well supported the idea of his Guru, Swami Rāmakrishna Paramahamsa that the service or man is the service of God. In his view, a man can see God, after worshipping the whole nature. This way, it is evident that the think-tank of Hinduism penetrated by Vivekānanda has no room for the feeling of caste, creed or community. That is why, it is liked and appreciated throughout the World. It is the social philosophy of oneness and one human kind.

At the metaphysical level, Vivekānanda was a great believer of liberation (Mokṣa), which he considered attainable through meditation. In his opinion, meditation is a great source of supreme bliss and it is a great inner stregnth. This view of Swami Ji influenced the West and particularly America, since his Chicago visit.

Karman and Brahman, are not contradictory in the philosophy of Swami Ji, instead of, they are co-existing and co-ordinating. In this regard, the following words of Vivekānanda, are most significant :

"*It may be that I shall find it good to get outside of my body, to cast it off like a disused garment. But I shall not cease to work. I shall inspire men every where, until the World shall know that it is one with God.*"

---

1. The complete works of Swāmī Vivekānanda, vol. II, p. 105.

He further says that only he lives a real life whose heart is substrated in Brahman and hand is engaged in action :

Hastaḥ karmaṇi saṃsaktaḥ cittaṃ brahmaṇyadhiṣṭhitam,
Niyataṃ yasya tasyaiva janma janmeti mematiḥ.

To focuss on the point of religion, at the outset, it would be appropriate to say that the religion, if practised properly, is a pathway to attain the reality, Mokṣa. It is through religion that one can purify his heart, which is a pre-condition for the realization in vedāntic view. The chief propounder of Advaita-Vedānta, Śaṅkarācārya clearly presented his Vedāntic ṭenet of one soul and said that there is no difference between Brāhmaṇa, Kṣatriya and so on and in them all, there is one Ātman. The Śaṅkarite view is fully capable of unifying the whole humankind and is the only proper way of integrating the whole nation.

Needless to say that the Vedānta or the philosophy of Advaita, which generally advocates the one soul theory is the best known thought of humanistic philosophy can be said as the soul of national integration. It is because the national integration is based on oneness of mankind irrespective of caste, creed, community or colour within the territory of nation. It will not be out of place to mention that the above idea of oneness especially preached by the Advaitins is not only the root of the integration of a nation but also the international integration. Regarding the oneness or non-duality, the essence of national integration, it will not be to exaggerate, that all creatives in the field of Sanskrit literature of Dharmaśāstra, ethics or polity, which directly or indirectly preach or indicate the spirit of nation's integration, have in their integrational background the aforesaid sense of non-dualism of the Vedānta or the Upaniṣadic thought. To illustrate, if Manu says that a person does not commit Adharma, if he has the idea of oneness of mankind, if in the Mahābhārata, it is mentioned that in pleasure and pain and in desirable and undesirable state, a man should see others like himself and if Sugata preaches the concept of non-violence to preach that in all there is one Ātman, then nobody would kill or harm any one; then there is found the idea of one soul tenet of Advaita in the background of above mentioned examples.

How the idea of oneness of the Vedic, specially Upaniṣadic period which is the backbone of national integration, was interpreted by Vedāntins like 'Śaṅkarācārya is to be observed. Here, it may be pointed out that the above idea of the oneness of soul was doctrinized by Advaitins like Śaṅkarācārya, according to whom all the differences and distinctions are apparant only and the reality is Ātman or Brahman. Thus the thought does not leave any place for the big social evil of Casteism or Communalism. The whole purpose of Vedāntin is to obtain the knowledge of the one-self—

Ātmaikatvavidyāpratipattaye sarve vedāntāḥ prāra bhyante. B.S.S.B. 1.1.1

Śaṅkarācārya, the great exponent of Advaita, clearly refutes the evil thinking of difference between Brāhmaṇa, Kṣatriya etc. (Apeta brahma kṣatrādibhedam) Regarding the evil of Casteism Śaṅkarācārya clearly says that the creation of caste is based on Upādhi, the Ajñāna :

Nānopādhivaśādeva jātināmāśramādayaḥ,

Ātmanyevāropitāstoye rasavarṇādibhedavat. Ātmabodha.

The secular and socio-political implications of Advaita Vedānta are also very much significant. In this regard, the Gītā says that for whom the duality or difference does not exist and who have equal view for all, are engaged for the welfare of all.[1] Śaṅkarācārya also says that those who are in peace, work for the welfare of whole world :

Saṃyatendriyāḥ sarveṣāṃ bhūtānāṃ hite ānukūlye ratā ahiṃsakā ityarthaḥ.

1. Śāṅkarabhāṣya, B.G.V. 25.

It is interesting to note that the guidelines given by Sarvajñātmamunca prominent post-Śaṅkaravedāntin that the serve of equality and truth is the best wealth of Brahma-jñānin, can be suitably successful for the resurrection of the modern day society and for inculcating the cultural values and also to achieve accordingly the result of common harmony;

Naitādṛśaṃ brāhmaṇasyāsti vittaṃ yathaikatā samatā nityatā ca.

—Mokṣadharma, 16.9.45.

It is futile to interpret that because the Vedānta advocates the only reality of Brahman, there can not be a place any sphere for the worldly behaviour or treatment; on the ground that the Advaitins like Śaṅkarācārya never support the view of empirical reality (vyāvahārika sattā) Here Vidyāraṇaya also may be quoted who says that the worldly behaviour is not opposed to the knowledge of ultimate reality or Brahman :

Tattvavittvaviro-dhitvāt laukikam samyagācaret.

—Pañcadaśī, Dhyānadīpa,

Likewise, giving importance to householders, Mādhavācārya says that all fruits ultimately depend on the tree of house holder :

sarvaṃ phalam gehapatidrumāśrayam.

—Śaṅkaradigvijaya, 14.10?.

He also says that what is necessary is the purity of mind. It is immaterial, whether one is a Samnyāsin or a house holder : Mano-viśuddho gṛhī bhavedvāpyuta maskarī vā.

—Śaṅkaradigvijaya, 13.5.

Furthermore, to support the reality of this world, Sarvajñātmamuni says that in this very life, the experience of Vedāntic, grea t sentences like. Aham brahmāsmi, is possible. He writes : Atraiva janmani bhavedapavargadāyi vākya prasūtamanubhūtiphalāvasānam.

—Saṁkṣepaśārīraka, III. 349.

Thus it becomes clear that the Vedānta is very much meningful for fullsided progress of mankind and national integration and today's world of narrowness and hatred based on casteism and the menace of communalism.

The culture imbibed in Vedāntic concept of Ekātmavāda has only the remedial measures which can uproot the social evils of the day which are a big hindrance in the path of national development. As indicated earlier, the Vedāntic culture based on the nondual philosophical tenet of the Advaitins has a capacity of uniting the whole mankind in one thread, the way of Vasudhaiva kutumbakam. It teaches the lesson of "Live and let live" others and further it advocates a Dharma, which does not come in the way of the followers of other Dharma, "sa dharmaḥ yo na bādhate dharmam" Vevekānanda too followed the above mentioned thought, laying more and more stress on the practice of Vedāntic view in life. For knowing the Reality, Swamiji adopted the Christianity and Islam and found that a true religion is always for the good of society. To Swamiji, there was no meaning of outward showyiness, like dress. To illustrate, once, in America, an American pulled his turban from his backside, then Vivekānanda told him that the dress does not matter so much, because it is one Ātman In all, irrespect of dress or any other outward consideration and we all are one. On this, the American apologised to Swamiji, for his misbehaving.

The essence of Vivekānanda's religion and philosophy was the service of humanity which he learnt from his guru, Shri Rām Krishna Paramahaṁsa. He thought that as a samnyāsin, he had to dedicate himself to the service of God, but God is to be revealed through humanity. In his opinion, religion is the backbone of Indian nation. He totally disagreed with the view of foreign critics that religion has been a hindrence in the way of Indian progress and development.

He interpreted that Indian culture was created and sustained by the twin ideals of renunciation and human service which formed the core of Hinduism. Being a practical Vedāntin, Vivekānanda advocated that is is better first to remove ignorance and poverty than to attempt for teaching metaphysics to empty stomachs.

In a sense, Vivekānand was a personification of faith and firmness. For this, an incidence, while Swamiji was in the United States, may be referred to. Once, when Swāmiji could not get food in the whole day, for having no money and was sitting under a tree in the forest at night, he saw a tiger, approaching him, but he did not move at all and sat firmly thinking that his body atleast will be used by hungry animal and left himself entirely in the hands of God. Whatever the reason may be, the tiger turned its head and went off in another direction. Swamiji spent the whole night meditating upon God and in morning, he felt a new surge of power. He always faced hardships and difficulties with calmness and courage. One day, while in America, he had no shelter, he spent the whole night in an empty Rail wagon, in the yard. When he went to Chicago, to participate in the Parliament of religions, he had no credentials to present and therefore he was worried about his attending it. To see him perplexed, Dr. J.C. Wright, a Professor of Greek at Harvard told him "To ask you Swami, for credentials is like to question the Sun about is right to shine."

At Chicago, in the Parliament of Religions, in the gathering of seven thousand people, presenting the true picture of Hinduism Vivekānanda said that it never comes in the way of other religions and in his view, all religions are the different pathways for achieving the same truth. Quoting the scriptures, he said :

"As different streams, having their sources in different places, all mingle their water in the sea, so, O Lord, the different paths which men take through different tendencies, various thoughts they appear, crooked or straight, all lead to Thee."

Summing up the shape of religion he said : The Christian is not to become a Hindu or a Buddhist, nor is a Hindu or Buddhist to become a Christian. But each must assimilate the spirit of the others and yet preserve his individuality and grow according to his own Law of growth. If the Parliament of religions has shown any thing to the world, it is this : "It has proved to the world that holiness, purity and charity are not the exclusive possessions of any Church in the world and that every system has produced men and women of the most exalted character. In the face of this evidence, if any body dreams of the exclusive survival of his own religion and the destruction of the others, I pity him from the bottom of my heart and pointout to him that upon the banner of every religion will soon be written, in spite of resistence : 'Help and not fight', Assimilation and not Destruction', 'Harmony and Peace and not Dissension."

Swami ji's performance in the Parliament of religions, where the presented Hindu religion in the form of international brotherhood, was par-excellence. Regarding it, the Boston Evening post said : He is a great favourite at the Parliament from the grandeur of his sentiments and his appearance as well. If he merely crosses the platform he is applauded; and this marked approval of thousands he accepted in a child like spirit of gratification without a trait of conceit."

In fact, it is one of the outstanding traits of Americans to draw out the latent greatness of other people. We can say that the discovered America discovered Vivekānanda and made a gift of him to India and the world.

In Vivekānanda's composite philosophy, there is no water tight division between religion and philosophy, as earlier also mentioned. To materialists, he showed the path of metaphysics and spiritualism. Swami ji being familiar with the arguments of materialism as with those of Advaita philosophy, showed the western people that their much wanted western science could not answer the most vital questions of life and being, that their immutable laws, so much talked of had no outside exietence apart from the human mind that the very idea of matter was a metaphysical conception and that it was much desired metaphysics, upon which ultimately rested the very basis of their materialism with an irresistible logic. Swami ji demonstrated "that their knowledge proved itself incorrect not by comparison with that which was true, but by the very laws upon which it depended for its basis; that pure reason could not help admitting its own limitations and pointed to something beyond reason; and that rationalism, when carried to its last consequences, must ultimately land us at something which is above matter, above force, above sense, above thought and then consciousness, and of which all these are but manifestations."

Secondly, the uphil task for Swāmīji was to remove the ignorance, superstitution and perverted ideas about religion in general and Hinduism in particular. Commenting once on Hindu religion, he said :

"No religion on earth preaches the dignity of humanity in such a lofty strain as Hinduism, and no religion on earth treads upon the necks of the poor and the low in such a fashion as Hinduism. Religion is not at fault but it is the Pharicees and Saducees."

For Vivekānanda, Vedānta and Hinduism were one and he found Hinduism quite imparallel as earlier also said, It would be true to say that in Hinduism, he wanted to see the real shape of mutual help and co-existence, peace and harmony a state of casteless society and a decent humane. His philosophy of religion was universial and therefore he had a co-ordinating view regarding all religions of the world. He thought that God, as ultimate god of all faiths, is their in most essence.[1]

Leaving a final note on the Vedāntic Hinduism advocated by Vivekānand, it may be said that by discarding materialism, he never supported the idea of its total avoidance, instead of, he gave it due consideration, but keeping in view the supremacy of spiritualism which was based on ethical and moral human values as well as the idea of one human kind.

1. Vivekānanda, by Swāmi Nikhilānand, Calcutta, p. 119, 120.

Sāṁkhya Elements in the Mahābhārata

Being an eye to see the reality, philosophy is as old as the human being whatever way and albiet in an indoctrinized manner. It Is because curiosity to know about the creator of the universe, the universe and its experiencer has been the subject of human mind, since its origin. The three have been the basics of Indian philosophy and have been seriously introspected and studied in different systems of Indian philosophy. It may also be mentioned that although there has been an effort all most in all the systems of Indian philosophy to explain the state of ultimate or reality, nevertheless it has remained a vexing problem and thus indescribable. The Encyclopaedia of Religion and Ethics rightly says : "The ultimate is some thing cognized and contant fact in all over conception. In it, and through it, is every thing. It is unconditioned and indescribable."[1] In Sāṁkhya, the ultimate is the state, in which the Prakṛti and Puruṣa are known as separate and not attached to each other and this is the state of Jñāna.

The Sāṁkhya thought which has beed elaborated in the Mahābhārata, the Bhagawadgīta and the Sāṁkhyakārikā of Īśvarakṛṣṇa has its sources in the Saṁhitās and the Upaniṣads. In the Ṛgveda, the Mantra, Ekam Sad Vipra Bahudhā

---

1. ERE Vol. I, pp. 137 f.
   See also, Ram Murti Sharma's paper, Ultimate principle in Śaṅkara's philosophy, published in "Ultimate in Ancient Indian Thought and discipline," Bombay, 1991.

Vadanti, for some scholars, is a base of the Sāṁkhya theory of causation, the Satkāryavāda. However I do not agree with this view, because the Vedāntins find the said mantra as the origin of their Sadvāda or the Brahmavāda. As far as the Upaniṣads are concerned, on the basis of the following mantras and like wise, the germs of Sāṁkhya thought may be guessed :

Ajāmekām lohitaśuklaKṛṣṇāṃ vahvīḥ prajāḥ sṛjamānāṃ sarūpāḥ.[1]

Māyāntu prakṛtim vidyānmāyinantu maheśvaraṃ[2]

It is argued on the basis of the above references that the Sāṁkhya thought has its origin in the Upaniṣads. S.N. Das Gupta says, "There are also passages in the Śvetāśvatara and particularly in Maitrāyaṇī from which it appears that the Sāṁkhya a line of thought had considerably developed and many of its technical terms were already in use.[3]

The references noted by Dr. Das Gupta are as follows :

1. Indriyebhyaḥ parāhyarthā arthebhyaśea param manaḥ. Manarastu parā Buddhir buddherātmā Mahān Paraḥ. Kaṭha III. 10.
2. Yonimanye prapadyante śarīratvāyadehinaḥ. Sthāṇu-manye nu samyānti yathā karmayathā śrutam. Śveta, V. 7.
3. Guṇānvayo yacha phalakarma kartā Kṛtasyatasyaiva sa copabhoktā.

   Sa Viśvarupstriguṇastrivartmā Prāṇādhipaḥ sañcaratisvakarmabhiḥ. Śveta, V. 7.
4. Anguṣṭhamātro ravitulyarūpchsaṁkalpāhankāra samanvitoyaḥ.

   Buddherguṇenātmaguṇena caivam Ārāgra-mātro hyaparopidṛṣṭaḥ. Śvet. V. 88.
5. Kṛyāguṇairātmaguṇaica teṣām S-amyoga heturaparopi dṣṣṭaḥ 7-Śveta 1.3 Śvet. 5.12.

6. Arāmekām. Śvet. 4.5
7. Te dhyānayogānugatā upaśyan devātma Śaktim svaguṇair-nigūdhām.
   Yaḥ Kāraṇāni nikhilāni tāni Kālātmayuktanyadhitaṣṭhatyekaḥ. Śvet. 1.3.

Let us examine the above mentioned references and see how far they justify the Sāṁkhya origin in the Upaniṣads. In reference i, the Triguṇātmikā Prakṛti (Ajā) has been generally taken by scholars related to Sāṁkhya. But there may be a counter argument that does the Vedānta not admit the Prakṛti as Triguṇātmikā or Mayā and beginningless (Anādi) and this is why the Vedāntins have quoted it for supporting the concept of Māyā or Avidyā, generally.[1] So to say on the reference ii, Śaṅkara, the commentator interprets the Prākṛti as the Māyā Śakti of Iśvara.[2] The references have been referred to by Das-Gupta as said above, to justify the Thesis that the Sāṁkhya line of thought had considerably developed and many of its technical terms were already in use.[1] As far as the 1st reference is concerned, in it, the senses have been mentioned as the lowest and Ātman as supreme. I do not think it helps to propound Sāmkhya in the Upaniṣads. However the terms "Buddhi" and "Mahān" may be taken similar to the Buddhi and Mahat principle of the Sāṁkhya doctrine. But this has no specification. The II reference also is irrelevant regarding the propounding of Das Gupta. It only says that people get their birth on the basis of their deeds and their Vijñāna, the knowledge.[3] As regards the third reference, the term Triguṇa can be said as parallel to Sāṁkhya views. So

1. Jivagatājñānanam samaṣṭyabhiprāyeṇa tadekatva vyapa deśaḥ "Ajāmekāmityādi śruteḥ, vedántarā. (EB 1 Delhi)
2. Iśvarasya Māyā śaktiḥ prakṛtiḥ, S.B. Śvet, up. 4. 10.
3. Yathā Karma yad ṛājyam Karma tad yathā Karma yair yās dṛs-aṃ Karma ih a janmani Kṛtaṃ tad Vaśenetyetat. tathā yathā ś-rutm yādṛsamca Vijñānamupārjitam tada-nrūpame Vaś-arīram prapadyante. S.B. Kaṭha.upa. 5.7.

also in the forth reference, the terms "Ahaṁkāra" and "Buddheḥ" are also found in the Sāṁkhya system. The fifth reference, which says that the Dehin Ātman takes many sthūla and sūkṣama forms due to his good and bad deeds, can not be specially linked to Sāṁkhya system It is also relevant to Vedāntic view point. About the sixth reference also, it may be said that it also applies to Vedānta, as indicated above. As far as the seventh reference is concerned, it is also not specially connected to Sāṁkhya and therefore it can be said that these references in no way advocate or indicate the Sāṁkhya view specifically. There are some who are fond of making flat statements like, there is satkāryavāda, in chāndogya (vi 2.1.) and they find it in the use of the word, Sat, there in. They may be asked, if the word Sat is not applicable to Advaitic Sat such of men analysts attention may be drawn to the fact the principle of Sat and Asat both have been refuted in the beginning of creation.[1] Here in, not to go in to much details, it may be sufficient to say that the Ṛgveda, by the aforesaid refutation of Sat and Asat, indicates the Anirvacanīyatā of the basic reality which is pro-vedāntic. It needs no elaboration that the Vedas and the Upaniṣads contain the Vedāntic ideas in their origin.[2] Sadānanda, a later Vedāntin rightly e dorses the Vedāntic view to mention "Vedānto Nāmopamṣat pramāṇam". To my view; it appears that Brahman is the central idea of Vedānta of the Upaniṣads and in them especially in the chāndogya, its treatment, clearly makes a pillar—like base for the Advaitic tenet which was fully enunciated by the great Advaitin, Śaṅkarācārya. But along side, it may also be mentioned that in the Upaniṣads, the word, Brahman has been used for other meanings too like sacrifice, the power of sacrifice, through which the desired result can be achieved.[1] This is simply to impress that there

1. Nāsadāsīt no, sadásīt tadānīm, R.V.X. 129. 3.
2. Vede Vedāntaḥ supratiṣṭhitaḥ, Mukti upa I.9

is no thought of Sāṁkhya as such in the Upaniṣads, but the dominent views there in, are Vedāntic decidedly. However it may be agreed that the Upaniṣads contain the seed like ideas of the six systems of Indian philosophy as well as Buddhism.

As far as the epic Mahābhārata is concerned, it may be said at the outset, that the Sāmkhya views expressed by Caraka (78 A.D.) are similar to those mentioned in the Mahābharata. It may also be admitted that the Śaṁkya elements Prevalent in the Mahābhārata are bound to be of a theistic nature, because of the theistic character of the Epic philosophy. Secondly the Sämkhya elements in the Mahābhārata, are found in two ways, i.e. I-attributed to Pañca-śikha, the disciple of Āsuri and II-the independent views. Regarding the identity of Pañcaśikha, it is necessary to mention that Pañcaśikha of the Mahābhärata seems to be different from Pañca Śikha of the traditional Pañca-Śikha cult. For example, the two views of Sâṃkhya attributed to Pañcaśikha in the Mahābhārata (XII. 219 and XII. 318, 96-112) are different. According to XII. 219, the account of sāṃkhaya agrees with the system of sāṁkhya as propounded by Pañcaś kha.

But contrary to it, in 318m 96-112, Pañcaśikha recognises thirty principles. However, there is no doubt that the Sāṃkhya elements prevalent in the Mahābhārata are quite identical with the well-known later Sāṁkhya views, with a few exceptions. In Sāṃkhya philosophy, Prakṛti and Puruṣa are the mcst dominent principles and in the Mahābhārata also they find a prominent place. The distinction between Prakṛti and Puruṣa has been clearly explained in the Aṇu-Gitā Like the twenty-four principles

1. See, Hillebrandt's article, 'BRAHMAN" in Encyclopaedia of Religion & Ethics.

of Prakṛti, which are the objects of Knowledge, Puruṣa is subject of knowledge (Jña) and thus, is the twenty-fifth principle.[2] As regards release, it is the state of realizying a distinction between spirit and matter.[3] In the Sāṁkhya Kārikā also, the twenty-five principles have been accepted and the Puruṣa has been mentioned as Jña).[4] As regards release, it is also the same as described in the Sāṁkhya-Kārikā.

The plurality of souls (पुरुष बहुत्वम्) is not possible, after realising the distinction between Puruṣa and Prakṛtl and it is justified only in the state of union of Puruṣa & Prakṛti. The Mahābhārata says that in the state of aforesaid distinction of Puruṣa and P.akṛti, the soul returns to the twenty-sixth principle of Īśvara.[1] The Prakṛti resolves in to Puruṣa, time to time. The Mahābhārata says that the self is like the spider which limits a web. The self sends out the Guṇas Sattva, Rajas and Tamas from itself.[2]

Pañcaśikha's eleaboration of Sāmkhya is much similar to that of caraka. Caraka and Pañcaśikha both admit Avyakta as ultimate truth, while in later Sāmkhya, Prakṛti has been mentioned as the ultimate. Like Caraka, Pañcaśikha says that the Guṇas—Sattva, Rajas and Tamas, are the good and bad qualities of mind. Unlike Vedānta, Prakṛti is different from self and it is Prakṛti which creates. But it always

1. Aṇu Gītā, xiv. 508.66.
2. Mb. xii. 306, 39, 40.
3. Mb. xii. 307. 20.
4. Vyaktāvyaktajña-Vijñānāt Sāṁkhya Kārikā 2.
5. Evam tattvābhyāsānna me nāhamityapariśeṣam. Aviparyayād Viśuddhaṃ Kevalamutpadyate jñānam, S.K. 4.
6. Mb. xii. 307. 20.
7. Mb. 314.12.

remains the control of Puruṣa.[3] The other way, it can be said that spirit brings activity in creative elements and thus it is akin to them.[4] Thus, indeed, all activity rests in nature and it is all productive and therefore to consider Puruṣa as active is false. This idea is very well-known in the Sāṁkhya Kārikā.[1]

The Aṇu Gītā mentions the Puruṣa as Kṣetrajña and body as Kṣetra. It evinces that all activity belongs to Kṣetrajña, the influence self.[2] The same view is also found in the Bhagawad Gītā. It may further be added that the stage of multiplicity is justified, till the Puruṣas are in union with nature. As soon as they realize their distinction from nature, they attain the stage of inner self. This stage of Puruṣa denotes the twenty-sixth principle of Sāṁkhya. This Puruṣa realises its own self in this state and then it has no connection with Prakṛti.[3] Now it is clear that this Puruṣa is different from the Puruṣa who is in bondage with nature.[4] Thus there remains no ground for the confusion regarding the Puruṣa in bondage and the liberated Puruṣaa. But this confusion is visible in the Saṁkhya Kārikā, where in, the distinction of the two is not clear. Here it may be said that this twenty-sixth principle of self realization brings the Sāṃkhya of the epic nearer to the Yoga system of Patañjali which very much admits the Puruṣa—Viśeṣa Īśvara.[1] But it may also be indicated here that Sāṃkhya and the Yoga are not the same

1. Mb. 314. 12.
2. Mb. 315. 8.
3. Tasmāccaviparyāsāt riddhhaṃ sākṣitvamasya puruṣasya, Kaivalyaṃ mādhyasthyaṃ draṣṭṛtvaṃakartṛbhāvaśca. S.K. 19.
4. Aṇu Gītā, xiv, 50. 8 ff.
5. SK. 64.
6. Aṇu Gītā, xii. 3:0,2), 26; 351, 2,4.

totally because, while Sāṃkhya is mainly based on reasoning the essence of the Yoga system rests in religious and Yogic practices. Also the process for attaining the release in Yoga is different from Sāmkhya.

The three qualities, Sattva, Rajas and Tamas, which are the constituents of nature are the prominent elements of Sāṁkhya and they are said to be the fetters of the Puruṣas and are very well discussed in classical Sāṁkhya. The Mahābhārata also treats them richly. The Aṇu Gītā says that it is through the ramp of nature that Puruṣa enters the darkness and the two are connected like the fly and the big leaf and the fish and water.

But as far as the final release is concerned, according to the Aṇu Gītā, the Puruṣa attains it after recognising the distinction between itself and Prakṛti. This is the stage, when all intermixture of Puruṣa and Prakṛti is ceased.

The Aṇu[1] Gīta makes three categories of men on the basis of the three qualities and they are Sāttvikas, Vyāmiśras and the Vaikārikas. The Sāttvikas are those in whom the quality of goodness is seen, the Vyāmiśras are those in whom the Rajas and Tamas, desire and indifference are mixed and the Vaikārikas are those in whom, the quality of indifference always prevails. Thus they never possess the quality of goodness. The Aṇugītā[1] also in accordance to the three aforesaid qualities of goodness, desire and indifference presents a classification of beings, Those who possess the quality of goodness, they advance to the world of gods, those who possess the quality of desire, remain in the world of men and those who possess the quality of indifference, fall in the world of beasts and plants.

---

1. Aṇu Gītā, xii. 348.
2. Aṇu Gītā, xiv. 36-38.

The idea of Sattva, Rajas and Tamas was first found in the Maitrāyaṇi,[2] a later Upaniṣad & after the epic in the Sāmkhyakārikā.[3]

Regarding the development, the Aṇugita (xiv. 40-42) mentions that the great self is produced from the Avyakta and from it, the individuation. The five elements are produced from individuation. The qualities of sound etc. and the five vital airs are produced from the five elements The eleven organs arise from the individuation.

Describing about the functioning of senses, mind and intellect, it is said in the epic that the senses present the data, the mind (Manas) raise is doubts and the intellect (Buddhi) is the deciding organ.[1] In Sāṁkhya-Kārikā also the idea about the three is prevanlant.

This way, and in many other ways, the clear base of classical Sāṁkhya and particularly the elements explained in in the Sāṁkhya Kārikā are found in the epic, Mahābhārata, but there are certain things, which are contrary. For example, the significant principle of Tanmātrās, explained in the Kārikā is not prevalent in the Mahābhārata. As regards the evolution, the epic mentions the theory like this : The five elements are avisesas, because they possess only their own nature and nothing specific (Viśesa), while the Viśeṣas possess the specific qualities, because they also contain the qualities of other elements, In the epic, another theory also is found which mentions that rather is

1. Tamo vā idamagra āsīdekam,........etad rūpam vai rajas......eta vai sattvasya rūpam, Maitrāyaṇī upaniṣad, v. 2.
2. S-attvaṃ laghuprakāśakamiṣṭamupaṣṭambhaKam calañca rajaḥ, guruvaraṇakameva tamaḥ pradīpavaccārthatovṛttih. S.K. 13.
3. Aṇugītā, xii. 275, 17; 235, 17.

the lowest which evolutes air and so on and thus the last is earth. The quality or the qualities of the last are found in the next. Both the theories have their original base in the Taittirīyopanisad.[1] According to the epic, the Visesas spring from the gross elements and the gross elements are directly derived from the absolute as said in the Taittirīya Upaniṣads.[2] It is because of the following to the Upaniṣadic test of the absolute that the Mahābhārata Sāmkhya has been mentioned as the seśvara sāṃkhya. It is also because of the same that the Sämkhya of the epic becomes nearer to the Yoga of Patañjali who finds a suitable place for Īsvara in his Yoga system,[3] Further more, in the epic the vital airs are described with a little significance.

There seems to be a mit gation and clash between the two theories prevalent in the epic i.e. (i) The actions are conditioned by the actions of previous life and (ii) the theory of human action and free will—and also the idea of devotion to God and his power of saving people.[4] If according to the theory of Karman if one reaps the result of his actions, then where remains the scope for the power of God to save people.

The epic Sāṁkya also mentions the two ways of the Gods (Devas) and Fathers (Pitṛs) through which people are said to achieve the Brahmaloka & get rebirth respectively. According to the third category, one takes the rebirth as a beast or a plant or the punishment of going to hell. Also in the Sāṁkhya Kārikā, this view is clearly found.

As to say on the tenet of Mokṣa, the Mahābhārata mentions two theories. According to one theory, the individual self attains the final knowledge of Brahman, which results in

1. Taittirīyoponiṣad iii. 4.1 ii. X. 1.
2. Yato vā imāni bhūtāni jāyante.
4. See, E.W. Hopkinś, article, JRAS., 1906, pp. 581-93.

supreme bliss through the means of perception, inference and scripture and the practice of Yoga. This theory is very much like the Advaitin's and so does not much owe to Sāṁkhya. The other theory, on the other hand, pleads the real knowledge to experience distinction between the spirit (Puruṣa) & the Prakṛti. As the Mahābhārata says, this is the final state of sp rit, in which the spirit becomes free from individuality and all consciousness.[1]

The twenty-fifth spiritual principle along with the teachers of Sāṁkhya, Jaigi savya, Aritā Devala, Parāśara, tars agaṇya, Bhṛgu, Śuka, Gautama, Pulastya, Sanat Kumāra, Śukra and Kaśyapa, is also found in the Mahābhārata.[2]

In the Mahābhārata, Pañcaśikha's system has been elaborated in detail.[1] But it is not connected to Sāṁkhya, at all, rather it is Vedāntic in its approach. Therefore a reference to Pañcaśikha, as a Śaṁkhya teacher in the Upaniṣad is quite controversial. Either he can be taken as sage[2] or a propounder of Sāṃkhya, who describes the Sāṃkhya thoughts with an inconsistency. If at all he is admitted as the Ācārya of Sāṃkhya, in that case he will be dated much earlier to 500 A.D. the date of Mahābhārata, which does not seem to be reasonable. The same contro versy is found regarding Kapila and Sanat Kumara etc. who were the divine beings and two whom certain philosophic ideas were ascribed.

It is interesting to note, as Oldenberg hints, that in early Buddhist texts, there is found the name of

1. Mahābhārata, xiv. 47.8.68. See also Keith, Sāṃkhya system, p. 45.
2. Mahābhārata, xiii, 319. 59.

1. MB xiii 219.
2. Taka Kusu, Bulletin de Ecob Franchaise d' Extreme orient, iv. 57 ff. TUXEN, Yoga, p. 14.

Pañcaśikha. But this similarity is accidental and this has nothing to do with the Pañcaśikha of epic.

Finally adjudicating the position of Epic Sāṁkhya, it may be concluded that it contains the Sāṁkhya elements based on the older Upaniṣads, like the Bṛhadāraṇyaka and Chāndogyopaniṣad and the later Upaniṣads like the S-vetāśvatra. It is because of this that the Sāṁkhya of the Mahābhārata is a mixture of the Brahman and Prakṛti-tenets of the Upaniṣads. Therefore it will be unfair to say that the Sāṃkhya of Mahābhārata is a full system and that the system existed even before Mahābhārata. Thus, here my disagreement with Garbe's view is clear which holds that this ingenuous system was in vogue before the rise of the epic.[1] Obviously the aforesaid view gets full support from Dahlman who thinks that it is the epic Sāṁkhya which represents the development of the unsystematic teachings of the early Upaniṣads.[2] Not only Sāṁkhya, but also the other five Āstika Darśanas, Nyāya, Vaiseṣika, Yoga, Pūrva-mīmāṃsā and mainly Vedānta, as well as Buddhism to a certain extent, have their origin in the Upaniṣads.[3] Regarding the Sāṁkhya of Mahābhārata, Keith seems to be right when he says: "but in the epic, as far as we can judge, it is still without some of the more characteristic of its minor doctrines, and has not achieved the completeness and subject to its main conceptions, clarity of outline which mark its classical form.[4]"

1. Garbe, Sāṁkhya Philosophie, pp. 54-59.
2. Sāṁkhya Philosopie (1902).
3. See A.E. Gough, Philosophy of the Upaniṣads. Ranade, Philosophy of the Upaniṣads. Deussen, Philosophy of the Upaniṣads.
4. Keith, The Sāṃkhya System, p. 62, Delhi, 1975.

The Bhagawadgitā : A guide to humankind

The Bhagawadgītā, which is from the Bhīśmaparva of the Mahābhārata, is an essence of the Upaniṣads, as the following verse says ;

सर्वोपनिषदो गावो दोग्धा गोपालनन्दनः ।
पार्थोवत्स : सुधीर्भोक्ता दुग्धं गीतामृतं महत् ॥

The Gītā is a bast guide to whole of human kind, with regard to religious and human code of conduct and for the attainment of peace in this world as well as supreme bliss or emancipation. It is the manual of duty and manliness. The seven hundred vreses in eighteen chapters of the Gītā, (1) the Arjunavisādayoga, (2) the Sāṃkhya yoga, (3) the Karmayoga, (4) the Brahmayajña praśaṃsā, (5) the Karma-saṃnyasayoga,)6) the Dhyānayoga, (7) the Jñāna-vijñāna yoga, (8) the TāraksBrahmayoga, (9) the Rājā-vidyā Rajaguhya-yga, (10) the Vibhūti yoga, (11) the Viśvarūpa-darśana, (12) the Bhaktiyoga, (13) the Kṣetra-Kṣetra-jñayoga, (14) the Guṇatraya-vibhāga-yoga, (15) the Puruśottama yoga, (16) the Daivāsura-sampad-vibhāga-yoga, (17) Śraddhā-traya vibhāgayoga and (18 the Mokṣa saṃnyāsa yoga, also indicate about tne religious, philosophical and social contents of the Bhagawadgītā. Ācārya Viṇoba Bhāve calls the Upaniṣads as grandmother and the Gītā, as mother.

The philosophy of Karman propounded in the Gītā is the key to success of life and happiness. It is the philosophy which teaches to stop worrying and start living. The Gītā teaches the performance of Karman without having the desire of its result and this is said as the Niṣkāma-Karmayoga.[1]

Through its teachings to Arjuna, the Gītā guides to humanity that one should not be attached to an unjust deed. It is really difficult to judge that what is right and what is wrong.[2] In this regard, the Gītā presents a soloution to say that God, who is Antaryāmin, exists in the heart of every body and therefore every body is directed by the inner voice to walk on the right path but it is the individual ego who even knowing the right path takes the wrong way, because of delusian. Therefore the Gītā teaches that a man should verywell decide about the karman before its preformance. Furthere more inaction is never the lesson of the Gītā, but it teaches a man to be detached in action and not from action. As a matter of fact, the story of the Gītā begins with the delusion and attachment because of which Arjuna fears from fighting with the Kauravas, his family members. The Gītā says that for a Kṣatrīya, dutiful fighting is his just deed.[3] Indeed the Gītā teachhs us to give up attachment and delusion and tnus Arjuna after listening to the lessons of Śri Kṛṣṇa, says, "my delusion is no more."[4]

Bhakti also is a significant aspect explained in the Gītā. A deep and unparallel love to God is Bhaktī.[5] Śāṇḍilya, in his Bhaktīsūtra defines Bhakrī as the supreme attachment to God (Parānuraktirīṣvare) In the Bhāgawata, there is a mention of the Navadhā Bhaktī, the nine types of Bhakti are :

---

1. कर्मण्येवाधिकारस्ते मा फलेषु कदाचन ।
   माकर्मफलहेतुर्भूर्मा ते सङ्गोऽस्त्वकर्मणि । B.G. 2.47
2. किं कर्म किमकर्मेति कवयोऽप्यत्र मोहिताः । Gītā, 4.16.
3. धर्म्याद्धि युद्धाच्छ्रेयोऽन्यत् क्षत्रियभूस्य न विद्यते ।
   Bhagawadgītā, 2.32
4. मोहोऽयंविगतोमम, Bhagawadgītā, 11.1, 18.74.
5. See, Bhaktisūtra, 1.1 and Swapneśvara's, Comm.

Śravaṇa, Kīrtana, Smaraṇa, Sevā, Arcana, Vandana, Dāsya, Sakhya & Ātma-nivedana. According to the Bhagawadgītā[1] faith (Śraddhā) is the base of Bhakti & Jñāna, both. A Bhakta, completely devotes his Karmans to God and dedicates himself to Him, He meditates upon Him and worships with full concentration and therefore it is by the grace of God that the Bhakta crosses the ocean of death[2] and attains Mokṣa. The Gītā says that God can be attained, by whatever way a person adopts. It may be the path of Karmayoga or Bhakti-yoga or Jñānayoga. The Gītā stresses more on giving up the desire for the result of the Karmans and says that Jñāna is superior to Abhyāsa.[3] Dhyāna is superior to Jñāna and to give up the desire for the result of Karmans, is superior to Jñāna.

Mentioning the characteristics of a Bhakta, the Gītā says that a Bhakta, envies to none and treats friendlines with all and is pathetic to those who are in suffering. He has no ego and no attachment and for him pleasure and pain, both are equal. He is tolerant.[4] Śrīkṛṣṇa further says that who is allways contented, selfcontrolled, fully devoted to Ātman and who dedicates his heart and mind to me, he is dear to me.[5] Defining further a Bhakta, the Gītā says that by a Bhakta, the world is never troubled nor the Bhakta is troubled by any one and thus who is away from the feeling of pleasure and

1. श्रद्धावाँल्लभते ज्ञानम् । Bhagawadgītā, 4.39.

2. येतु सर्वाणि कर्माणि मयि संन्यस्य मत्पराः ।
अनन्येनैव योगेन मां ध्यायन्तुपासते ।। Gītā, 12.6
तेषामहं समुद्धर्ता मृत्युसंसारसागरात् । Gītā, 12.7

3. श्रेयो हि ज्ञानमभ्यासात् ज्ञानाद् ध्यानं विशिष्यते ।
ध्यानात् कर्मफलत्यागस्त्यागात्शान्तिरनन्तरम् ।। Gītā, 12.12.

4. Gītā, 12.13.

5. Gītā, 12,14.

anger, fear and perplexity, is dear to lord.[1] The Gītā says that who is desireless, sacred, expert in performing his duty, fearless and who does not perform his actions with a desire, is dear to Lord.[2] He is dear to Lord, who is not happy to get a particular object, who is not perplexed to get an undesirable thing, who is not perterbed, if he does not get his desirable and who has no longing at all.[3] The Gītā further says that only he is dear to Lord, who takes badwords and praise, as equal, who is sillent, who is contented with whatever he gets, who has no house and who has fixity of mind.[4] Likewise, the Mahābhārata, mentions the characteristics of a Brāhmaṇa, thus :

Yena Kenacidācchannaḥ yena kenacidāśitaḥ.

Yatrakvacana śāyī syāttam devā brāhmaṇaṃ viduḥ.[5]

It may be pointed here that for Śrīkṛṣṇa, a Bhakta and a Jñānin, both are equally dear.[6]

The Dhyāna yoga propounded in the sixth chapter of the Bhagawadgītā, is not less important than the Karmayoga, Jñānayoga and the Bhaktiyoga. Moreover the Gītā mentions the place of the yogin, a follower of Dhyāna yoga, superior to a Tapasvin, a Jñānin and a Karmin.[7] As far as

1. Gītā, 12.15.
2. Gītā, 12.16.
3. Gītā, 12.17.
4. तुल्यनिन्दास्तुतिमौनी सन्तुष्टो येन केनचित् ।
   अनिकेत: स्थिरमतिर्भक्तिमान् मे प्रियो नर: ॥
5. Mahābhārata, Śāntiparva, 245.12
6. प्रियों हि ज्ञानिनोऽत्यर्थम् । Gītā, 7.17.
   भक्तास्तेऽतीव मे प्रिया: Gītā, 12.20
7. तपस्विभ्योऽधिको योगी ज्ञानिभ्योऽपि मतोऽधिक: ।
   कर्मिभ्यश्चाधिको योगी तस्माद् योगीभवार्जुन ॥ गीता, 6.46

the meditation (Dhyāna) is concerned, for it, concentration of mind is essential as also has been described in Yogasūtra. The Cītā mentions about the physical postures (Āsanas) Prāṇāyāma and Pratyāhāra etc., as the means of the concentration of mind.[1] The Gītā further teaches that a person should entirely devote his concentrated mind to the Lord, Śrīkṛṣṇa.[2] It is to be noted that the yogic description in the sixth chapter of the Gītā is prevalent in the Śvetāśvatara Upaniṣad. The Gītā further mentions two types of the yogins, the Yukta and the Yuktatama. That who, is contented with Jñāna& Vijñāna, is Kūṭastha, has a control over the senses, and for whom, the clod, stone and gold, are equal, is Yukta. Among the yogins, who has constant devotion to the Lord ŚrīKṛṣṇa, with faith, is the Yuktātmā.[3]

Let us now take in view the Jñānayoga concept of the Gītā. At the outset, it may be said that like the Karmayoga and Bhaktiyoga, the Jñānayoga has its significane in the Gītā. The Jnānayoga of the Gītā is the advocate of Ātmajñāna. To Arjuna, who is afraid of fightirg with the Kauravas, Śrikṛṣṇa tells about the eternity of Ātman and says that Ātman is unborn and eternal[4] and therefore it can never be killed. As the Gītā says, a Jñāninlives at a lonely place, like forest or the bank of a river, eats light, has a control over heart, speech and body, remains engaged in meditation[5] and has an attitude

---

1. B.G 6.11 – 18
2 मनः संयम्य मच्चितो युक्त आसीत मत्परः । B.G. 6.14
3. योगिनामपि सर्वेषां मद्गतेनान्तरात्मना ।
श्रद्धावान् भजते यो मां स मे युक्ततमो मतः ॥ B.G. 6.47
4. अजोनित्यः शाश्वतोऽयंपुराणो न हन्यते हन्यमाने शरीरे ॥ Gītā, 2.20.
5. ज्ञानी त्वात्मैव मे मतम् Gītā, 7.18

of detachment.[1] A Brāhma jñānin is always happy and thus he never suffers from any grief. He has no desire and to him, all are equal.[2]

As said earlier, God, as an Antaryāmin exists in the heart of all and He, being Sākṣin, witnesses the actions of all. He is approver, protector and an experiencer.[3] Here it may be argued that how God, as an approver approves The tundesirable actions of a man. Therefore as Śaṅkara says God is like an apqrover and not an approver.[4] As regards the question of experiencing of God, it may be said that God is an experiencer through Jīva, the individual soul.

The Gītā consider the Jīvanmukta as a Sthita-prajña and says that when the mind of a person is fixed in Samādhi, he becomes a Sthitaprajña and the Sthita prajāa is a Jīvanmukta and none-else. When a person after giving up his all desires, is fully contented in his Ātman, he becomes a Sthitaprajña.[5] According to the Gītā, the Sthitaprajña is a Muni, who is unpurturbed in the state of pain, has no desire in the state of happiness, and has no attachment and anger and who has a fixed mind.[6] The Gītā further says that a Sthitaprajña has no attachment to his body and nor to his life. He is neither happy to get the good and nor unhappy to get the bad. (Śubhāśubha-parityāgī). Thus the ĀtmaJñānln, after

1. Gītā, 18.52
2. समः सर्वेषु भूतेषु । Gītā, 18.54.
3. उपद्रष्टाऽनुमन्ता च भर्ता भोक्ता महेश्वरः । Gītā, 13.22.
4. अथबा अनुमन्ता कार्य-कारण प्रवृतिषु स्वयं अप्रवृतः अॅप प्रवृत इव तदनुकूलो विभाष्यते तेन अनुमन्ता । S B. Gītā, 13.22.
5. प्रजहाति यदा कामान् सर्वान् पार्थ मनोगतान् ।
आत्मन्येवात्मना तुष्टः स्थितप्रज्ञस्तदोच्यते ॥ Gī .ı, 2·55.
6. Gīṭā, 2.56, 5.28.

giving up his desires, when lives desirelessly and has no attachment and ego, attains the supreme peace, the Mokṣa.[1] This is also said as the Brāḥ ni state.[2]

Through various ways and means, the Gītā teaches to be an ideal man. As the Gītā mentions, a Karmagogin, a Bhakta or a Jñānin is an ideal man. By teaching the philosophy of Niṣkāma Karma Goga to Arjuna, Lord Śrīkṛṣṇa has taught to Arjuna, the way of being a great personality. Accordingly a person who performs his actiods without having any desire or inclination is a man of wisdom.[3] His actions are burnt in the fire of knowledge. An idea Karmagogin is alwuys satisfied and he has no attachment with the result of actions and thus he has no dependence on the worldly affairs. Therefore, although he performs ųis actions, he does not do them with any inclination.[4] A person, who ha snō aspirations, has controlled his mind and body, has all sourccs of the enjoyment and performs only bidily acticns, never commits a sin, he is indeed an ideal man. The ideal man iss satisfied with what he get s, is above the clash of pleasure and pain, without the feeling of hatred and jealousy, eual in success and failure and is never in bondage of Karman.[5] The Gītā says that a person who has no feeling of

1. विहाय कामान् सर्वान् पुमाँश्चरति निस्पृहः ।
निर्ममो निरहङ्ककार : स शान्त्तिमधिगच्छति ॥ Gītā, 2.71.

2. एषा ब्राह्मी स्थितिः पार्थ नैनाँ प्राप्य विमुह्यति । Gītā, 2.72.

3. यस्य सर्वे समारम्भाः कामसङ्कल्पवर्जिताः ।
ज्ञानाग्निर्दग्धकर्माणं तमाहुः पण्डितं बुधा ॥ B.G. 4.19,

4. B.G. 4.20

5. निराशीर्यतचित्तात्मा त्यक्तसर्वपरिग्रहः ।
शारीरं केवलं कर्म कुर्वन्नाप्नोति किल्विषम् ॥ B.G. 4.21

6. B.G. 4,22,

hatred and jealousy and has no desire for any thing, he is really a Saṃnāsin, for, he, being without likes and dislikes, is liberated from the worldly bondage.[1] A person, who performs all his actions dedicating to God, is never effected by any sin and he is like a lotus leaf which is never effected by the water on which it rests.[2] Therefore the Yogins perform their actions without any attachment and they perform them for the purification of their heart.

To maintain the sense of equality, Samatva Yoga is the essence of the philosophy of the Bhagavadgītā. The Gītā says that whose mind is settled in equality, he is liberated in this world[3] and thus he is the Jīvanmukta. A person should not be pleased to achieve the desirable and nor he should be perplexed to get the undesirable and thus he is the liberated who has a fixed mind.[4] Indeed an iddeal man, according to the Bhagawadgitā, is a practical man and a Karma Yogin, who has his base of spiritualism. It is evident by the fact that in the end of each chapter of the Gītā in the Pusp.kā, the Gītā has been mentioned as "Brahmavidyā and yoga-śāstra".[5] It shows that the Gītā is both, the Brahmavidyā as well as the Yogaśāstra, which contains the philosophy of Karmayoga. As the main propounder of the philosophy of Karmayoga, the Gītā teaches to be engaged in action and to worship the Lord, through action.[6] It is thus that Arjuna is

---

1. ज्ञेयः स नित्यसंन्यासी यो न द्वेष्टि न काँक्षति ।
   निर्द्वन्द्वो हि महावाहो सुखं बन्धात् प्रमुच्यते ॥ B,G, 5.3
2. B.G. 5.10
3. इहैव तैर्जितः सर्गो येषां साम्ये स्थितं मनः । B.G. 5.19
4. न प्रहृष्येत् प्रियं प्राप्य नोद्विजेत् प्राप्य चाप्रियम् । B.G. 5.20
5. ब्रह्मविद्यां योगशास्त्रे ।
6. यतः प्रवृत्तिर्भूतानां येन सर्वमिदंततम् ।
   स्वकर्मणा तमभ्यर्च्य सिद्धिं बिन्दति मानवः ॥ B.G. 18.46

advised to fight with the Kauravas, but remembering the Lord.[1] Now it is clear that the spiritualism of the Gītā never imparts the teaching of escapism, instead of, it teaches a man to become a spiritualist Karmayogin. The Gītā also teaches the society to maintain the order of varṇāśrama, based on the division af quality (Guṇa) and Karman.[2] As earlier also has been said, an ideal man, according to the Gītā, is a Sthitaprajña[3], a Bhakta[4] and a Guṇātīta.[5]

Thus being the essence of the Upanisads, on the basis of their spiritual philosophy, the Bhagawadgītā presented the philosophy of Jñāna, Dhyāna, Bhakti and Karma, as an application to the new circumstances which arose at the time of the Mahābhārata and not only this, the Gītā provides a solution in all circumstances which a person may face in different ways. Truely speaking, the Gītā is a pathshower to the theistic, the spiritualist and the Karmayogin.

---

1. मामनुस्मर युध्य च । B.G. 8.7
2. चातुर्वर्ण्यं मया सृष्टं गुणाकर्मविभागशः । B.G. 4.13
3. See, B.G. 2.55-72.
4. B.G. 12-13-19.
5. B.G. 14-21-27.

Indian Saints after the Buddha

The Encyclopaedia of Religion and Ethics defines a saint, thus : The popular the saint, as a being of eminent holiness, and especially as one of the immediate desciples of the Master, holds a prominent place in early Buddhism. The term is used occasionally as a technical translation of Arthat, but this does not correspond exactly with the usual ideas of the saints of history.[1] In Chinese, for saint, the term is "SHEN JENG" which means "Holy man"[2] or sage.[3]

Defining saint it is explained in the dictionary of comparative religion that "one who had attained such perfection of wisdom and virtue that be completely fulfilled his destiny as a human being, was perfectly in harmony with cosmic law and this formed a trinity with heaven or earth. The stress is laid as much on intellectual as moral attainment. Such perfection entitles the saint.

The Gītā says that a saint never makes a difference between a friend and a foe and thus for him all are equal. Tulasīdāsa, mentioning the charaeteristics of a saint describes that the heart of a saint is as soft as butter. According to the Rāmacaritamānasa, tolerance is the great quality of a saint. Therein, Tulasidāsa mentions that the saints tolerate the hard and bad words of the bad people like the

---

1. ERE Vol. XI, P. 49.

2. A Dictionary of Comparative Religion, N.Y.P. 548.

3. B.G.VI. 4.

4, Santa hṛdaya navanīta samānā.
Kabā Kavina para kabā na jānā. Rāmācaritamanaṣa,

mountains tolerate the hurt caused by raindrops.[1]

In India, the history of saints starts from the Ṛgveda, wherein the supreme reality has been described as "Sat" and that it is described by the "Vipras" in many ways.[2] The "Vipras", here, can be understood as the saints. Whatever the period or circumstances may be, the saints are allways inquisitive to reality, may be through Jñāna or Bhakti or mysticism or any other approach. In the Ṛgveda, there is a big number of the Ṛṣis like Medhātithi, Śunaḥśepa. Dīrghātāmā, Gṛtsamada, Viśvāmitra, Vāmadeva, Atri, Bhāradwāja and so on. As the word Ṛṣi means.[3] they were the reavealers of truth and thus more than the saints.

Not only the Ṛṣis, the Ṛsikā saints are also prevalant in the Vedas. For example, among the Vedic Ṛṣikās, Vagāmbhṛṇī[4], Indrāni,[5] Śraddhā,[6] Lopāmudrā,[7] Urvaśī,[8] Ghoṣā,[9] Sūryā,[10] Viśvavarā,[11] Apālā,[12] Juhū,[13] Dakṣiṇā[14] and

---

1. Bunda aghāta sahen giri jaise
   Khala ke vacana santa sahen taise. Ramacarita-mānasa.
2. Ekam sad viprā bahudhā vadanti. R.V. 1.164.46,
3. Ṛṣayo mantradraṣṭāraḥ.
4. R.V. 10.125.
5. R.V. 10.145.
6. R.V. 10.51
7. R.1.179.
8. R.V. 10.95
9. R.V. 10.39.6
10. 10.85.9
11. R.V. 5.88
12. 8.90
13. 10.109
14. 7-10. 107

Yamī[1] are prominent. Of them, Ambhṛṇi is the daughter of the Ṛsi, Ambhṛnī and Sāyaṇa considers her as Brahman and as substratum (Adhiṣṭhāna). She says that in her, the world is super-imposed as silver is superimposed on the conch shell.[2] Here Vāgāmbhṛṇī is characterized like a Vedāntin saint. So also the Ṛṣikā, Śradhā is the symbol of faith, a great virtue of a saint and Ghoṣā, a sufferer of leprosy is Brahmavādinī. Juhū, the wife of Bṛhaspati also is Brahmavādinī.

Thus it is found that in the Saṃhitās, the male and female saints lead mostly a spiritual life which leaves a great impact on society. But the Vedic saints were not the propagators of religion or spiritualism a like the saints of post-vedic times. Their approach was much more individual.

Like the Samhitās, in the Upaniṣads too, there are male and female saints like Naciketā, Yājñyavalkya, Satyakāma, Sanaka, Sanandana, Sanatknmāra, Gārgī, Maitreyī and many others, As is evident by the story of five boons of Naciketā and several other examples, the Upaniṣadic saints directly or indirectly advocate the stress on spiritual awakening and the final mission of liberation. As the Upaniṣadic philosophy enunciates, Brahman is the finality and the world is Māyā. The Upaniṣadic philosophy also advocates the concept of Jīvanmukti, which means that a person even after the realization of Brahman can live in this world living a saintly life. As a matter of fact, this concept of Jīvanmukti can be said as the basic concept of a saint, who lives his life without any selfish motive and is allways engaged in the welfare of society, (Śāntāmahān) to loka-hitam carantaḥ).[3] A Jīvanmukta saint lives in this world like the

---

1. R.V. 10.10.
2. Mayi hi sarvam jagat śuktau rajatamiva adhyastam dṛśyate. S.B.RV. X. 125.
3. Sa cakṣuracakṣuriva, Sakarṇa akarṇa inva.

lotus leaf which exists in the water, but is never touched by it. Likewise the Jīvanmukti saint also lives in this waking world but is never afflicted by the worldly miseries.

In the Gītā, which is the essence of the Upaniṣads, there are found three types of saints and they are Karmayogins, Jñanayogins and the Bhakti-yogins. A person, who performs his right actions, without having any desire for their fruition, is a renounercer and a Karma-yogin and not a firelessman or who does not work.[1] The Gītā further mentions that a Karmayogin saint never desires for worldly objects and for the result of the Nitya, Naimittika and Kāmya Karmans and thus he is a renouncer of all purposes Sarvasaṁkalpa-Saṃnyāsin. Further, a saint is that who has controlled his body and is placid, his sovereign spirit is fixed in itṣelf in cold. I heat, pleasure or pain, honour and dishonour.[2] Again who has equal judgement for the lover, friend, enemy, the indifferent, the neutral, the hateful the kindred, the good and the sinful too, he is distinguisheds. The Gitā says that the Karma-Jnāna-yogin is a Sthitaprajña, who cast off, all his desires and is satisfied in his state of Ātman.[3] A saint, a Sthitadhī Muni is never perturbeḍ while in

1. Anāśritaḥ Karmaphalam Kāryam Karma Karoti yah,
Sa Saṃnyāsi ca yogī ca na niragnirna cākṛyah.
Bhagawadgitā, VI.I.

2. Yadā hi nendriyārtheṣu na Karmasvnuṣañjate.
Sarvasamkalpasaṃnyāsīyogāruḍhastaducyate. B.G.VI. 4.

3. Jitātmanaḥ praśāntasya paramātmā samāhitaḥ;
Śitoṣṇasukh-duḥkhṣu tathā mānāpamānaycḥ. B. 9 VI. 7.

4. Suhṛnmitrāṛyudāsīna madhyasthadveṣyabaṇdhuṣu.
Sādhuṣvapi ca pāpeṣu samabuddhirviśisyate. B.G.VI. 9.

5. Prajahāti yadā kāmān Sarvān pārtha manogatān,
Ātmanyevātmanā tuṣṭaḥ sthitaprajñastaducyate,
B.G. 2.55.

trouble and he has no desire in happiness. Of such a saint, attachment, fear and anger are allways finished.[1]

The saints who are the followers of Bhakti, according to the Bhagawadgītā, dedicate their each and every action to God.[2] For the Bhakta saint, abuse and praise are equal and he is silent and satisfied with whatever he gets. He has a restraint on his speech, has no fixed residence and has a fixed mind and such a saint is dear to God.

Thus, by the above mention, it is evident that that the Bhagawadgītā presents a clear picture of a saint which is based on the Vedāntic cult and the point of view of determinate worship prevalent in the Upaniṣads. These two Upaniṣadic versions are also the results of the Jñāna and Karman aspects of the Saṃhitās. One way or the other the portrayal of saintliness continued in the Purāṇic literature with its broadness and vividity. In this regard, the names of great saints like Vyāsa, Vālmīki, Nārada, Vaśiṣṭha and Viśvāmitra, Jamadagni and Atri may be mentioned. Even in this period, female saints like Śabarī are significant. Furthermore, Janaka is a great example of those saints, from the Ramāyana. who lived their life as Jīvanmukta, being Videha, having no attachment with his physical body.[3]

---

1. Duhkheśvanudvignamanaḥsukhesu vigataspṛhaḥ.
   Vītarāgabhaya—krodhaḥ sthitadhīrmunirucyate.
   B.G.II. 56.

   See also, yā niśā sarva-bhūtānam tasyām jagarti saṃ yamī. B.G.II. 69.

2. B.G. ix. 34.

3. Tulyanindā stutīrmaunī santuṣṭo yena kevnacit.
   Aniketoḥ sthiramatir bhakimān me priyo naraḥ.
   B.G. xii. 19.

The above portrayal of saints, in brief, in the Vedic and Purāṇic period, has a firm foundation of the philosophy of Śaṅkarācārya, a most prominent Jñānin saint of post-Buddha period, who established the tenet of Advaita or one soul, on the basis of his doctrine of Māyā, due to which Brahman is the only ultimate reality and the world is Māyā. He was the disciple of Govinda-bhagavatpāda, who consecreted Śaṅkarācārya, by giving him the toe of his right foot through the hole of the cave, in which he lived. On one side, he propound Brahman as the infinite reality and on the other he regarded the world as finite and phenomenally real. As a matter of fact, Śaṅkara's Advaita has been capable of uniting the whole world in one thread of Brahmanic reality and that is why it has been studied and experienced throughout in the east and west. Śaṅkara, the saint preached his tenet of Advaita by instituting the four Maṭhas, the Jyotirmaṭha, at Badarikāśrama, the Gobardhanamaṭha at Dwārikā and the fourth maṭha at Śṛiṅgerī, at the four corners of India. It may also be mentioned that the philosophical thought of Śaṅkarācārya is not only meant for an enquirer into Brahman or Mokṣa ; it also has a straight message for the nondiscrimination of cast and creed.

Returing the concept of caste etc., Śaṅkara says that the creation of castes is based on the adjunct and therefore false it is meaningless.[1] In nutshell, the sole aim of Śaṅkara's Vedāntic tenets is to propagati the concept of one soul in all which can be said in today's racial and political mate, a gateway to global unity. The above thought was advocated by the Vedāntin saint, Śaṅkarācārya roaming throughout India in 8th and 9th century (A.D).

It is necessary to note that the philosopher saint Śaṅkara

---

1. Nanopādhivaśādeva jātināmāśramādayaḥ;
Atmanyāropitastoye rasavarṇādibhedavat. Ātmabodha

was a follower of the path of Jñāna as well as Bhakti, His Saundaryalaharī as well as the stotras clearly support the above point of view and it was so that Śaṅkara was following the line of the Upaniṣans which founded the concept of indeterminate and determinate Brahman. Following Śaṅkara, a later Advaitin, Madhusudana Saraswatī also maintained the Bhakti-Viśiṣṭādvaita concept. Thus it is noteworthy that the concept of Jñāna and Bhakti is traceable from the Ṛgveda and which travelled its path through the Vedic texts, the Gīta, the Purāṇas etc. and it was a accordingly that if Śaṅkara found Advaita in the Brahma-sūtra of Bādarāyaṇa Vyāsa. Rāmānuja, Nimbārkā, Madhva & Vallabha & many others found the cult of Bhakti in the same Brahmasūtra and it was on the basis of the same that the four—great Ācāryas expounded the concept of Visiṣṭādvaitā, Dvaitā-dvaita, Dvaita and Śuddhādvaita, respectively. It is also to be kept in view that while Śaṅkara was mainly preaching that Jñāna is the means for Mokṣa, the Vaiṣṇava Ācāryas were of the view that the Sālokya, Sāmīpya, Sāyujya and Sārūpya moksa can be achieved through the path of Bhakti of Viṣṇu, the Bhagawān.

Now, it is clear that the Samnyāsin saints like Saṅkara, Sureśvara, Padmapāda, Sarvajñātma Muni, Amalananda, Vidyāraṇya, Madhusūdana, Brahmānanda, Ramādvaya, Śaṅkarānanda, Akhaṇḍānanda, Ramānanda and Mahādevā Saraswatī showed the path of Jñāna to society through their writing and discourses, time to time and the Vaiśvāṇara saints like the aforesaid propagated the easier path of Bhakti among the common people. These two paths shown by the Vedāntin and Bhakta Ācāryas were intellectual and there was, thus a need of bringing them to comman man and this great task was performed by the saints like Kabīra, Nānaka and so on. Now let us overview the contribution of these saints.

The saints like Kabīra, Nānaka, Dharmadāsa, Dādū,

Rajjaba. Sunderdāsa, Garībadāsā. Yārīsāhaba, Bullā Śāha, Bhīkha, Paltū, Malūkadāsa, Sahajo bāi, Dayābāi and Tulasī Sāhab propagated the path of Jñāna of the Vedāntins, while the path of Bhakti was preached by the Bhakta saints like Narasī, Tukārāma, Eka nātha, Sūra, Tulasī and Mīrā, by their writings like Sūrasāgar & Tulasī's Rāmacaritamānasa and by singing the songs (Bhajanas) full of the virtues of Bhagawan like Karuṇā and grace, Kīrtana and dancing, In Bhagawāṇ in devine love one with Bhagawāṇ Bhakti, being a great attachment to God and a unique love toward. Him is an easier apprach for a comman man and due to it, it became more popular among comman people. There has been a big number of Śaiva and Vaiṣṇava saints in southern part of India, Mahārashtra, Bengal, Assam, Kashmir and other parts of the country. For illustrating, the twelve Vaiṣṇava saints—the Ālāvaras[1] of south are well-known and they are : Poyage Alavara, Bhūtattālavāra, Peyālavara, Tirumandise Ālavāra, Nambihālavāra, Madhura Kavi, Kulaśekhara Ālavāra, Viṣṇuktīpari—Ālavāra, Godā Anaḍāla, Vipranārāyana tarādaradippoli, Munivāhana or Tirupanna and Tirumange-yolavāra. They were mostly all Tamilians[2]. They became made in the bhakti of Viṣṇu. and generally read the Viṣṇu saharanūma. These saints existed from 2nd century to 10th century A.D. There have been also some Śaiva-saints in south and in them twelve were prominent and of all them Tirunāna was most prominent. The period of prominent Śaiva saints, is 5th century to 11th century (AD). To go from one place to another was the nature of saints and therefore it was thus that because of the influence of southern saints, Maharashtra also created a big number of saints. Among the Maharashtra saints, Jñānadeva (1275 A. D) is foremost. He was the worshipper of Śrī Bhagawān

1. Parānuraktirīśvare, Śāṇḍilya-sutra.

2. See, J.S.M. Hooper, Hymn of Ālavāras. Introduction, P. 26.

Viṭṭhala, who is Viṣṇu. Nāmadeva, Tukārāma, Oñāneś-vara, Ekanātha, and Rāmadāsa were the mosi prominent saints of Maharashtra, In Bengal, the Sahajiyā school of Vaiṣṇava saints was prominent and the Vaiṣṇav saints like Jaideva, Vidyāpati, Caṇḍīdāsa, Dāmodara and Mahāprabhu-caitanya belonged to the same school. Chaitanya was a great devotee of Srīkṛṣṇa.

In Assam, there were two schools of Vaiṣṇava saints, the Mahāpuruṣiya and the Vabhuniyan. Saṅkara deva was the prominent saint of the former school, while Hari devand Gopāladeva were the Vaiṣṇava saints of the later school. There was also the Avadhūta school started by Dattātreya. Brahma-Purāṇa and the Mārkaṇḍeya Purāṇa describe much about Dattātreya. In Kashmir saints, Lāladeva (1500 A.D) is most prominent. As Griarsen finds Kabīra was influenced by the thoughts of Lāladeva. At the same time, there were some other schools of saints, known as, Valmīki, Pañcap-riya, Cistiyā, Suharāvardiya and Kādiriyā school. Taking into account, the Indian saints, we must refer to the Sūfī saints. The first sūfi saint was Abūhāsim. There were also some other Sūfī saints like Alagajjāli, Śekha Sādī and Jalaluddin Rūmī. The Sūfī saints mainly advocated the view that the spiritual love can be attained through worldly love.

Thus we find that the chain of saints in India, is con-tinuous and has been glittering with faith and shades of knowledge and devotion, which are allways full of human and godly love.

In present century too, there has been a galaxy of saints who devoted themselves for human awakening in Inḍia and outside and were revered in the whole globc. In such philosopher saīnts, Ramakṛṣṇa Paramahaṃsa, Vivekānanda, Aurobindo and Ramatīrtha are highly prominent. Swāmī

Rāma Kṛṣṇa Paramahaṃsa laid more stress on human service and Vivekānanda's emphasis was on practical Vedānta. Aurobindo was a Yogin who preached that the world is born of Ānanda (bliss) and living by Ānanda wheeling from Ānanda to Ānanda. Ānanda and Śakti, these are the two real terms of existence.[1] Among the raints of modern century, the names of Sister Ninveditā and the Mother of Pondicherry, are highly worthmentioning.

Furthermore Ācārya Vinoba Bhāve has been a most significant reformist saint of this century who, on Gandhian lines, started a crusade for the uplift of down-trodden and for creating a sense of equality in human beings. His main contribution is Bhūdāna yajña, under which he requested the rich Land lords to donate land to the poor people and he was successful in this plan. On the pattern of the Brahmasūtra of Bādarāyaṇa Vyāsa, he wrote the Sāmya sūtra to propagate the understanding of equality among all people. Also there have been many other great saints in India like Ramaṇa Maharṣi Śivānaṇda, Sain Baba and Deoraha Bābā. Deorāhā Bābā allways lived in a hut erected on four pillars at the bank of a river. Mother teressa also is a great saint of to-day who has been serving the downtrodden, the sufferers of leprosy and such other deseases and homeless to give them a very affectionate healing touch, in all parts of the country. In present days, there is one more prominent school of saints in India, known as Brahma Kumārīs' school. It is a unique school. It was started by Śiva Bābā. It has its branches all over the world and its headquarter is at Mount Abu, (Rajasthan), one of the beautiful places of the country, enriched with the luminous beauty of nature. The Brahma Kumārī organization has its one University in India, named as Īśvarīya viśvavidyālaya situated mainly at Mount Abu. The saints of this school allways wear white dresses. They propagate to awaken spiritual insight through

1. Yogic Sādhana, P. 83.

meditation and social and cultural understanding in society. There are also some other schools of saints in India like the Vāhīs'. These saints lay more stress on prayer and meditation. In Delhi, they have builtup a big & beautiful lotus temple, which is highly worthseeing.

Briefly, the Indian saints' objective is to create a sensc of enquiry in man for kn owing the spiritual and religious rcality, and to create a faith among people towards omniscience and omnipotence of God, and understanding that one has to reap the result of his Karmans, a belief that the performance of dnty is the man's first and foremost job and to create a sense of human service and fellowship in society. Generally the Bhakti and Jñāna, are the two main pathways of Indian saints.

BIBLIOGRAPHY

Abhiprāyaprakāśikā citsukhācārya		Madras Government oriental series, 1965.
Abhiprāyaprakāsikā : A study (Hindi),	Sharma, Priti	EBL Delhi 1994.
Advaita Vedānta	Sharma, Rammurti	EBL Delhi 1978.
Aitareya Brāhmaṇa,	Ānandāśrama series, Kashi.	
Aitareyāraṇyaka		Kashi
Advaita-siddhi	Saraswati, Madhusūdana	N.S. Bombay, 1937.
Aaitareyjāraṇyaka-paryālocanam	Mangal Dev Shastri.	
Aparokṣānubhūti	Śaṅkarācārya	Srirangam.
Arthasaṁgraha	Laugākṣibhā-skara	Delhi, 1973.
Bhagawadgītā		Gorakhpur, Gītā Press.
Bhāvaśuddhi	Ānandapūrṇa-muni,	Madras Government oriental Series, 1967.
Bhojavṛtti	Bhojadeva	Oriental Series Ajmer, 1961.
Brahmasiddhi	Maṇḍanamiśra	Madras Government Oriental Series, 1963.

Brahmasūtra-Śāṅkarabhāṣya	Śaṅkarācārya	Srirangam
Brahmasūtra—S.B.E.		Oxford, 1890.
Bṛahadāraṇyakopaniṣad	Ānandāśrama	Poona, 1927.
Chāndogyopaniṣad	Ānandāśraṁa	Poona, 1926.
Complete works of Svāmī Vivekānanda		Advaita Ashram, Calcutta.
Constructive survey of Upaniṣadic philosophy	Ranade	Poona, 1926.
Daivata Brāhmaṇa.		
Encyclopaedia of Religion and Ethics, vol. I.		
Gauḍapādakārikā	Gauḍapādācārya	Srirangam.
Glimpses of Vedānta	Sharma, Rammurti	EBL, Delhi, 1989.
Hari Sharma's Comm. on Śatapatha Brāhmaṇa		
History of Indian Philosophy, vol. I & II,		Dasgupta, S.N. Cambridge, London, 1940.
History of Vedic literature (Hindi),	Sharma, Rammurti	EBL Delhi.
Hymn of Ālavaras, Introduction	J.S.M. Hooper.	
Indian Philosophy, vol. I & II	Radhakrishnaan, S.	London, 1966,

Title	Author	Publisher
Indiche Studies	Weber.	
Journal of Royal Asiatic Society, 1906.		
Kaṭhopaniṣad,		N.S. Bombay, 1925.
Madhvasiddhānta-sāra.		
Mahābhārata,	Vyāsa	BORI Poona.
Mahānārāyaṇopaniṣad		Moti Lal Banarsi Das, Delhi.
Maitri Upaniṣad,		Poona.
Māṇḍūkyopaniṣad,		Mysore 1936.
Mimāṃsā,	Thadani, N.V.	Bharati Research Institute, Delhi, 1952.
Mukti Upaniṣad,		Motilal Banarasi Das, Delhi, 1980.
Muṇḍakopniṣad,		Motilal Banarasi Das, Delhi.
Nyāyasūtra	Gotama.	Kashi.
Pañcadaśī Vidyāraṇya,	Buddhi-sevāśrama,	Ratangarh, Saṃvat, 2011.
Pañcaviṃśa Brāhmaṇa,		
Praśastapādabhāṣya	Praśastapāda,	Chowkhamba, Varanasi.
Praśnopaniṣad,		Gita Press, Gorakhpur.
Religion and Philosophy of the Veda,	Keith, A.B.	Harvard Oriental Series, vol. 32.

Śaṅkarācārya and his doctrine of Māyā,	Sharma, Ram Murti	EBL Delhi 1993.
Śāṅkarabhāṣya, Gītā,		Gorakhpur, Gītā Press, Samvat, 2010.
Śaṅkaradigvijaya,	Mādhavācārya	Kashi.
Śāṅkhāyanāraṇyaka,	Ānanḍaśrama,	Poona, 1922.
Sāṁkhyakārikā	Īśvar Kṛṣṇa	Delhi, 1969.
Sāṁkhya philosophy	Garbe.	
Sanskrit Texts	Muir.	
Saṁkṣepaśārīraka,	Sarvajñātma-Muni,	Varanasi, 1924.
Sāṁkhya system	Keith, A.B.	
Satapathābrāhmaṇa Śāstradīpikā.	Eggeling's Translation.	
Sāyaṇābhāṣya	Sāyaṇācārya.	
Six Systems of indian Philosophy	Maxmuller	Calcutta.
Some Aspects of Advaita philosophy :	Sharma, Rammurti	EBL Delhi, 1985.
Śvetāśvataropaniṣad : Taittirīya Brāhmaṇa.	Ānandāśrama,	Poona, 1811.
Taittirīyopaniṣad,		Motilal Banarsi Das, Delhi.
Tātparyaṭīkā,	Udyotakara.	
The Hymns of Atharva Veda	Peterson,	

The Hymns of the—Ṛgveda,	Peterson	
The Hymns of the Sāmaveda,	Griffith R.T.H.	
The Principal Upaniṣads :	Radhakrishnan S.	
The Religion and Philosophy of the Atharvaveda :	Shende, T.N.	Poona, 1952.
The Vedānta :	Ghate	BORI, Poona.
The Vədānta philosophy,	Maxmuller, F.	
Ultimate in Ancient Indian thought,		Bombay, 1991.
Upadeśasāhasrī	Śaṅkarācārya,	N.S. Bombay, 1914.
Vākyapadīya :	Bhartṛhari	Poona, 1965.
Vaiśeṣikasūtra	Kaṇādā,	The Sacred Books of the Hindus, Allahabad, 1923.
Vedānta-paribhāṣā Dharmarajādhvarīndra,		Varanasi 1994.
Vedāntasāra	Sharma, Rammurti	EBL Delhi 1989.
Vedāntasidhānta-muktavalī	Prakāśananda	Acyutagranthamala, Kasi, 1893.
Vedic Mythology	Macdonell A,	

Vedic Reader	Macdonell, A.	
Viṣṇupurāṇa,		Calcutta.
Vivekacūḍāmaṇi	Śaṅkarācārya, Srirangam.	
Vivekānada	Nikhilānanda, Swāmī, Calcutta.	
Yajurveda-Saṃhitā,	Vedic Śaṃśodhanamaṇḍala, Poona.	
Yogavāśiṣṭha,	Vaśiṣṭha, N.S.P.	Bombay, 1937.
Yogasūtrabhāṣya	Vyāsa,	Varanasi, 1971.

INDEX

K

L

M

———

SOME OPINIONS

DR. S. RADHAKRISHNAN writes about his Ph. D. thesis on Śaṅkarācārya :

"Best wishes for the publication of the work which I hope will be read widely."

PROF. HAJIME NAKAMURA : (Tokyo, Japan), mentions him "one of the leading scholars of Asian religion and philosophy in India.

PROF. F. TOLA : (Argentina) describes him among the modern significant philosophers.

DR. B. L. ATREYA writes on his Ph.D. thesis, śaṅkarācārya : "Being a scholar of Sanskrit DR. Sharma has read Śaṅkara from his original Sanskrit works, and in forming his opinion he has been very careful and judicious. His exposition is simple and clear and criticism unbiased".

M.M. DR. UMESH MISHRA writes on his book, Advaita Vedānta : 'He had for the first time given a systematic exposition of the development of Advaita from the earliest times till upto date "

PROF. NELSON LUNG : (Director, Asian Research service Hong-Kong) : "you are among a selected group of scholars to be specially invited to join the International centre of Asian studies as a Fellow.

PROF. GERALD LARSON (California) writes on the book, Some aspects of Advaita philosophy : "The book, Some aspects of Advaita philosophy because of its clear and systematic presentation of the subtleties of Vedānta, will be especially welcome to the scholars of Advaita Venānta. It showes the eminence of Professor Ram Murti Sharma whom I consider one of the top most scholars of the field. As I also have seen at the International conferences, his deliberations have been of a very high calibre "

DR. RAJA RAMANNA :

"I am happy that a devoted and eminent scholar of Sanskrit particularly Advaita Vedāita, Professor Ram Murti Sharma, is being honoured by the galaxy of scholars from all over the world, to contribute their papers in different fields of Sanskrit learning. Professor Sharma has propagated Advaitic thought of Ādi Śaṅkarācārya throughout the world, through his deliberations in national and international seminars and conferences, lectures and his works, like Śaṅkarācārya, Advaita Vedānta, Some Aspects of Advaita Peilosophy & The Glimpes of Vedānta and his papers published in Various Journals, time to time." (Preface, Glory of knowledge., the Felicitation vol. of Prof Sharma.

PROF. JUAN MIGUEL DE MORA :

President, International Sanskrit symposium Mexico city. "He (Prof. Ram Murti Sharma) presented his paper on Dṛṣṭisṛṣṭivāda and also delivered a conference on Advaita philosophy. His papers were of very high calibre and he made an impression during the deliberations of the symposinm."

